The Revision Guide to AS and A2 Level Economics

James Keefe

anforme

© Anforme Ltd 2002

ISBN 0 907529 70 4

Anforme Ltd
Stocksfield Hall, Stocksfield,
Northumberland NE43 7TN

Typeset by George Wishart & Associates, Whitley Bay.
Printed by SPD Ltd, Gateshead.

CONTENTS

PREFACE

This revision book will prepare students for examinations in AS and A2 Economics. It covers most of the major topics that a student needs to know and, with the help of headings, bullet points and definitions, it sets out to provide a summary of the concepts needed for a successful revision programme.

Having said this, the book does not explain every topic from first principles. If you have not understood one of the major items in the book, then the revision material provided here will not offer a short cut to understanding and learning. You will need to go back to your textbook or teacher's notes for enlightenment.

The distinction between the concepts needed for AS and A2 varies between the different exam boards. At AS you should only revise the concepts that you have covered in your course. If you have any queries you should consult the specification for your examination board and ask your teacher for advice. The book is laid out in such a way that you should be able to pick out the concepts you have studied and use the notes as a cornerstone for your revision.

Good luck with your revision programme!

James Keefe

Chapter 1
INTRODUCTION TO ECONOMICS

One of the first questions students ask when they start a course in economics is why is there a need to study the subject? The simple answer is that there is a **basic economic problem** – there are only a limited number of resources available to satisfy our needs and wants. Thus economists must attempt to reconcile this problem of **scarce resources** and infinite **desires**.

WHAT IS SCARCITY?

This is a situation where there are only a limited number of resources available to produce goods and services. The **finite resources** used to produce output can be categorised in four ways. Collectively, they are called the **factors of production**:

▶ **Land** – the natural resources on the planet. These include produce obtained from oceans and rivers, as a result of a favourable climate. Minerals extracted from the planet, such as diamonds and aluminium, are also classified as land. The only major resource on earth that is not scarce is the air that we breathe. This is called a **free good**.

▶ **Labour** – human resources used to produce goods and services. In the UK, there are around 28 million workers involved in the production process.

▶ **Capital** – items used by labour in the production process. Examples include factories, machines, roads and computers. All these capital items allow the production of goods and services in future time periods.

▶ **Enterprise** – the individual, or group of individuals, who is prepared to take a risk and combine the three other factors of production.

WHY IS SCARCITY A PROBLEM?

On its own scarcity is not a problem. The basic **economic problem** only occurs because people who belong to society have needs and desires that exceed the availability of resources. In a developing country, inhabitants will first try to satisfy their **needs** and obtain food, clothing, shelter and work. Once they have fulfilled all their needs they will not be satisfied with this most basic standard of living. They will now wish to consume other goods and services.

Even in economically developed countries consumers are never satisfied. Technology means there is always a more up-to-date mobile phone or a brand new car model and, as a result, individuals invariably **want** something else.

The basic economic problem means decisions must be made by society, or by individuals, on three central economic questions:

1. What goods and services are to be produced?

2. How are they produced?

3. For whom are they produced?

OPPORTUNITY COST – THE NEXT BEST ALTERNATIVE FOREGONE

The problem of scarce resources means that choices have to be made. This is true for individuals, firms and governments who all have to make decisions about how to allocate resources.

▶ An individual does not have an unlimited income and must therefore make economic choices on a daily basis. This could be whether to buy a new CD player or a DVD player. Workers must also decide if it is worth sacrificing leisure time so they can earn extra income to raise their standard of living.

▶ Firms may have to decide whether to use profits to invest in new machinery or to increase dividends to shareholders.

▶ Governments cannot spend infinite amounts of money on public services. They may be faced with difficult decisions, such as whether to increase spending on the National Health Service or on Education.

Such choices nearly always involve a cost. For example, the decision to purchase the CD player means that the DVD player will have to be given up. This is known as **opportunity cost** and is defined as **the next best alternative foregone.**

PRODUCTION POSSIBILITY FRONTIERS (PPFs)

A **production possibility frontier** illustrates what an economy can produce using the resources of land, labour and capital. It is useful in explaining the concept of **opportunity cost**. Consider the example of an economy that allocates all its resources to providing either manufactured goods or services. This is illustrated in Diagram 1.1.

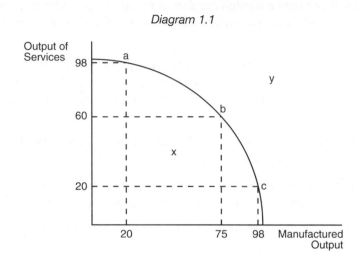

Diagram 1.1

▶ Points a, b, and c all lie on the PPF and show maximum production when all economic resources are **fully employed** and used **efficiently**.

▶ Point x lies within the frontier and illustrates a situation where the factors of production are not fully employed and/or are being used **inefficiently**.

▶ Point y is not yet attainable given the current level of resources in the economy.

The production possibility frontier can be used to illustrate **opportunity cost**. The concave shape of the frontier indicates that the opportunity cost of manufactured goods in terms of services increases as more manufactured goods are produced.

If the economy were to **specialise** in producing manufactured goods, increasing output from 20 units to 75 units would lead to a relatively small fall in the production of services from 98 units to 60 units. The **opportunity cost** of the 55 unit rise in manufactured output is the 38 units of services that have been foregone.

Specialising even further, and increasing manufactured output from 75 units to 98 units, leads to a relatively large fall in the provision of services from 60 to 20 units. The **opportunity cost** of this small 23 unit rise in manufactured output is the 40 units of services that have been foregone.

This increasing opportunity cost can be explained by the fact that not all resources are equally suited to the provision of manufactured goods and services. The factors of production used in increasing manufactured output from 75 to 98 units are far better suited to the provision of services and this explains why the output of manufactured goods only increases by a relatively small amount.

ECONOMIC EFFICIENCY AND PPFs

The PPF can be used to illustrate two types of **economic efficiency**. To be producing on a PPF all the factors of production must be fully employed and there must be productive efficiency.

Productive efficiency means that firms are combining the factors of production and producing goods and services at the lowest possible cost. To be operating on the PPF all firms must therefore be producing output at the minimum points on their average total cost curve (see Chapter 6).

Pareto efficiency occurs when no one can be made better off without making anyone else worse off. This concept can be applied to Diagram 1.1. If the economy is operating at point x it is possible to produce more manufactured goods and services by moving to point b. We can increase output from both industries without having to make any sacrifice. This indicates that any point inside a PPF is **pareto inefficient**.

If we move between two points that actually lie on the PPF it is impossible to attain more manufactured output without having to give up some services. A sacrifice has to be made. As a result, any point that lies on a PPF must be **pareto efficient**.

SHIFTS IN THE PRODUCTION POSSIBILITY FRONTIER

Diagram 1.2

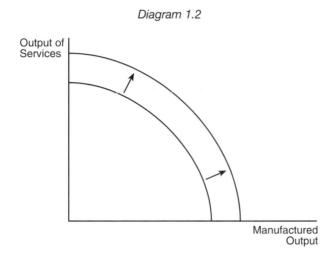

In Diagram 1.2, the PPF shifts outwards in parallel direction. This could have been caused by:

▶ An increase in the quantity of the factors of production – the shift may have originated from the discovery of new energy supplies, an increase in the active workforce or investment in new machinery.

▶ Improvements in efficiency or new technology – if there is an increase in the productivity of factors of production this will allow more output to be produced. The IT revolution of the last few years has caused the PPFs of many economies to shift outwards.

An improvement in new technology will not always cause a parallel shift in the PPF. For example, a new computerised production process will only impact on the manufacturing sector. The productive potential of the service sector will remain unchanged. This will lead to a shift in the PPF as shown in Diagram 1.3.

Diagram 1.3

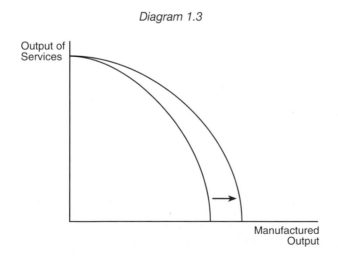

ECONOMIC STATEMENTS

There are two types of economic statements:

▶ **Positive Statements** – a statement which objectively describes the economy.

▶ **Normative Statements** – an opinion or view about what ought to, or should, be done.

For example, the UK's emissions of CO_2 are around 10% of that of the United States. This is a **positive statement** as it objectively describes a situation in the economy. If an economist argued that the US should dramatically reduce its emissions; this is a **normative statement** as it expresses an opinion.

Chapter 2
PRICE THEORY

In most **markets**, prices are determined by the interaction of market **supply** and **demand** for the good or service. There are many examples when **government intervention** aims to influence price and affect the **allocation of resources**. These are considered in Chapter 4 which examines applications of price theory.

EFFECTIVE DEMAND AND THE DEMAND CURVE

Demand in economics must always be **effective**. Only when a consumer's desire to buy something is backed up by a **willingness** and an **ability** to pay for it do we speak of demand. For example, many people would be willing to buy a luxury sports car, but their demand would not be effective if they did not have the means to do so. They must have sufficient **purchasing power.**

Demand is defined as the **quantity** of a good or service that consumers are **willing and able to buy at a given price in a given time period.** For normal goods there is an **inverse relationship** between the quantity demanded and the good's own price. This is illustrated in Diagram 2.1.

Diagram 2.1

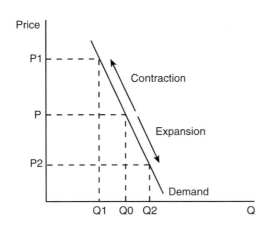

Diagram 2.2

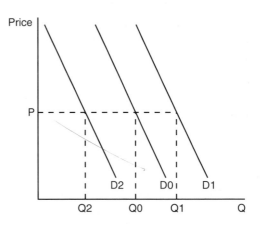

▶ A **change in the price** of the **good itself** causes a **movement** along the demand curve. For example in Diagram 2.1, a **rise in price** from P to P1 causes a **contraction** along the demand curve. Conversely, a fall in price from P to P2 leads to an **expansion** in quantity demanded. These movements along the demand curve are usually caused by shifts in the supply curve, although they might also be caused by the imposition of specific prices by the government.

▶ A change in one of the **conditions of demand** will lead to a **shift** in the demand curve. This is illustrated in Diagram 2.2. When the demand curve shifts to the right (D0 to D1) more is demanded at each and every price (Q0 to Q1). When demand shifts to the left (D0 to D2), there is a fall in demand for the product at each price level (Q0 to Q2).

CONDITIONS OF DEMAND

1. **Real income** measures the quantity of goods and services that a consumer can afford to buy. An **increase in real income** will cause the demand curve to shift to the **right** for the vast majority of goods that are classed as **normal**. However, some goods are **inferior** – this is where an increase in real income will cause demand to shift to the **left**. Examples of inferior goods include rice, potatoes, tobacco and bus travel. An increase in income will cause the demand for bus travel to fall, as commuters switch to superior modes of transport such as private motor cars or rail services. The impact of a change of income on demand is analysed further in Chapter 3 when we look at **income elasticity of demand**.

2. **Prices of other goods – Substitutes and Complements**

Substitute goods or services are those in **competitive demand** that satisfy a similar need or want. Examples include different brands of soap powders, or types of crisps or soft drinks.

▶ A fall in the price of a substitute good will cause demand to shift to the left. If there is a fall in local rail fares (a substitute for bus travel), demand for train services will increase, but demand for bus travel will shift to the left.

Complementary goods or services are those goods and services that are often consumed together. They are said to be in **joint demand**. Examples include DVD players and DVDs, tennis racquets and tennis balls and package holidays and travel insurance.

▶ A fall in the price of a **complementary good** will cause the demand curve to shift to the right. If there is a fall in the price of new and second hand cars, the demand for these products will expand, and the demand for petrol (a complementary) will shift to the right.

3. **Tastes and preferences** – tastes can be volatile, and often lead to a change in demand. A good example would be the large fall in demand for British holidays during the Foot and Mouth crisis. Fluctuations in consumer tastes can lead to big variations in demand at each price. This is particularly true for products that are fashionable for a very short period while there is a craze to purchase them. These goods are called **fads**. Examples include scooters and yo-yos.

   Standard demand theory assumes that consumer preferences are fixed – meaning that one person's preferences do not affect those of others. This is now being questioned. In many markets, the views of some consumers have an impact on the preferences of other consumers (either positively or negatively) – these feedback effects can mean that demand for certain goods and services becomes volatile and difficult to predict.

4. **Interest rates** – the level of interest rates affects the demand for many items, particularly 'big ticket' household durable goods (TVs, consumer electronics and dishwashers) and items typically purchased on **credit** (cars, home improvements and holidays).

   A rise in interest rates will reduce demand. Higher interest rates increase the incentive for consumers to postpone consumption and save their money instead. Higher rates will also increase the cost of loan repayments and discourage consumers from undertaking a purchase. Changes in interest rates also affect **consumer confidence** and therefore influence the willingness of consumers to commit themselves to major items of spending.

5. **Population changes** – a rise in population will shift the demand for most goods to the right. However, the age structure of the population is also important. The UK has an **ageing population** and, inevitably, the demand for products such as pensions, nursing homes and stair lifts will shift to the right.

6. **Advertising and Marketing** – a successful advertising or marketing campaign will shift demand to the right. This in itself makes the **price elasticity of demand** for the product more inelastic. Advertising seeks to **inform** (e.g. tell the market about new products; price changes; explain how a new product works, etc.), **persuade** (e.g. develop a consumer's brand preferences to encourage them to switch goods) and **remind** (keep a product in a consumer's mind). The effects of advertising on preferences should not be underestimated.

The importance of the "ceteris paribus" assumption

It is important to remember that the demand curve is drawn assuming **ceteris paribus**; that is, "all other things being equal". A change in any of the **conditions of demand** will result in a **shift** in the demand curve. Only a change in the **price of the good** itself will lead to a **movement** along the curve.

WHY DO DEMAND CURVES SLOPE DOWNWARDS?

SUBSTITUTION AND INCOME EFFECTS

The downward sloping shape of a demand curve can be explained by the **substitution** and **income effects** of a price change. Consider the following example. A fall in the price of bananas, a normal good, will result in an increase in demand. This increase in demand for bananas can be broken down into two effects:

1. **Substitution Effect** – the fall in the price of bananas means that they are now **relatively cheaper.** As a result the consumer will switch away from substitute goods such as apples, pears and peaches and towards bananas.

2. **Income Effect** – the fall in the price of bananas means that **the consumer's real income or purchasing power** has increased. This may encourage the consumer to purchase more bananas, although they could also buy more of other goods.

Most goods obey the law of demand and have a downward sloping demand curve. Some, however, do not, and in these instances there is a positive relationship between price and quantity demanded.

EXCEPTIONS TO THE LAW OF DEMAND

Some luxury sports cars, watches and clothes have an upward sloping demand curve because they exhibit a **'snob effect'.** A fall in the price of a luxury product that is consumed for **ostentatious reasons** may result in a fall in demand. This is because as the price of the product falls it loses some of its snob appeal and kudos and consumers will switch to more expensive and exclusive products. Goods that exhibit this snob effect are known as **Veblen Goods.**

Giffen goods are very inferior products on which low income consumers spend a high proportion of their income. When the price of these products falls, low income consumers are able to discard their consumption of these goods (having already satisfied their demand) and move onto superior goods. Thus demand may fall when price falls. This phenomenon now only tends to occur in developing countries with basic foodstuffs.

THE THEORY OF SUPPLY

Supply is defined as the **willingness and ability** of producers to supply output onto a market at a **given price in a given period of time.** There is usually a **positive relationship between supply and price.** As prices rise it becomes more profitable for existing firms to increase output and supply may be boosted further by the entry of new firms into the industry.

A change in the **own price of the good** (caused by a shift in the demand curve) results in a **movement along the supply curve.** A fall in price causes a **contraction.** A rise in price causes an **expansion.** This is illustrated in Diagram 2.3. A change in one of the **conditions of supply** causes a shift in the supply curve. When the supply curve shifts to the right more goods are supplied at each and every price. This is shown in Diagram 2.4.

Diagram 2.3

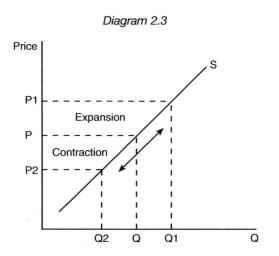

Diagram 2.4

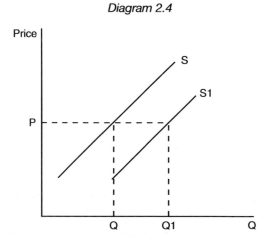

CONDITIONS OF SUPPLY

Any factor that raises the costs of production will shift supply to the left.

1. **Prices of factors of production** – raw materials, components and wage levels. A fall in the price of paper would shift the supply curve for a newspaper producer to the right as more output can be supplied at each price. In contrast, for a haulage company, higher fuel costs would cause supply to shift to the left because fuel is an essential raw material.

2. **Productivity of factors** – an improvement in labour productivity means that each worker will be able to produce a higher level of output. This will reduce **unit labour costs** and shift the supply curve to the right. The efficiency gains are usually passed onto the consumers in the form of lower prices.

3. **Indirect taxes or subsidies** – the introduction of VAT or additional excise duties on a good will shift the supply curve to the left. This is because taxes add to the costs faced by a producer. The supply curve of the insurance industry has shifted to the left following the recent introduction of the insurance premium tax.

   A **subsidy** encourages a producer to increase production. The grant or payment from the government will lower a firm's costs of production and shift the supply curve to the right. The supply curve of many agricultural commodities has been shifted to the left over the last decade following a reduction in subsidies from the European Union.

4. **Producer decisions** – The aims of a business can affect its supply decision. For example, if a firm switched from **revenue maximisation** to **profit maximisation** this would cause the supply curve to shift to the left (see Chapter 5).

5. **Technological advances** such as the developments in robotics and information technology reduce the costs of production and shift the supply curve to the right.

6. **Prices of substitutes** – a rise in the price of a substitute will cause supply to shift to the left. Suppose the price of parsnips rose, this would encourage farmers to increase the production of this particular root vegetable and reduce the supply of others such as carrots and turnips.

7. **Entry of new firms into an industry** – the entrance of new firms into an industry shifts the supply curve to the right and puts downward pressure on the market price (see Chapter 6 on **perfect competition**).

EQUILIBRIUM PRICES IN A MARKET

Equilibrium is defined as a state where the **market clears**, with no forces acting to change the equilibrium prices and quantities. It occurs when **demand equals supply**. This is shown in Diagram 2.5 (a) with the equilibrium price at P and the quantity traded at Q.

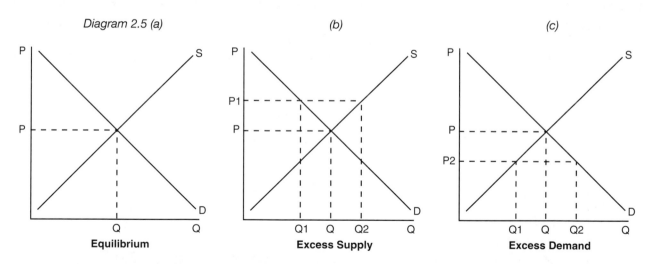

When there is a situation of **excess supply** or **excess demand** the market is said to be in **disequilibrium**. Forces are at work pushing the price and quantity back towards equilibrium. In Diagram 2.5 (b), when prices are at P1 there is **excess supply** (quantity supplied Q2 is greater than quantity demanded Q1) and firms will be forced to reduce prices in order to **shed stocks**. There will be an expansion along the demand curve and a contraction in supply until a new equilibrium is established at a lower market price P. In Diagram 2.5 (c), when the price is at P2 there is **excess demand** (quantity demanded Q2 is greater than quantity supplied Q1) and prices will be forced upwards as there is a **shortage** of the product. This causes an expansion along the supply curve and a contraction in demand until equilibrium is, once again, restored at price P.

Chapter 3
ELASTICITY

ELASTICITY OF DEMAND

Elasticity of demand measures the **responsiveness or sensitivity of demand** to a change in a variable that affects demand.

PRICE ELASTICITY OF DEMAND (PED)

Price elasticity of demand measures the responsiveness of **quantity demanded** to a change in the good's **own price.** The formula for the calculation of PED is:

Price elasticity of demand (PED) = $\dfrac{\text{\% change in the quantity demanded of good X}}{\text{\% change in the price of good X}}$

How is PED calculated?

Consider the following demand schedule for buses in a city centre.

Price (average fare)	Quantity of passengers per week
100p	1,000
60p	1,300
30p	2,275

Suppose the current average fare is 100p, what is the PED if fares are cut to 60p?

The **percentage change in quantity demanded** is equal to:

▶ the change in demand 300 (1,300 − 1,000) divided by the original level of demand 1000. To obtain a percentage this must be multiplied by 100. The full calculation is (300 ÷ 1000) x 100 = 30%.

The **percentage change in price** is equal to:

▶ the change in price 40p (100p − 60p) divided by the original price 100p. To obtain a percentage this must be multiplied by 100. The full calculation is (40 ÷ 100) x 100 = 40%.

These two figures can then be inserted in to the formula with 30% ÷ 40% = **0.75**.

Let us now consider the PED when the average fare is cut from 60p to 30p.

The **percentage change in quantity demanded** is equal to:

▶ the change in demand 975 (2,275 − 1,300) divided by the original level of demand 1,300. To obtain a percentage this must be multiplied by 100. The full calculation is (975 ÷ 1,300) x 100 = 75%.

The **percentage change in price** is equal to:

▶ the change in price 30p (60p − 30p) divided by the original price 60p. To obtain a percentage this must be multiplied by 100. The full calculation is (30 ÷ 60) x 100 = 50%.

These two figures can then be inserted into the formula with 75% ÷ 50% = **1.5**.

There are some important points worth remembering when calculating PED:

▶ The elasticity figure is a **real number**, not a percentage or fraction.

▶ The PED will **vary along a demand curve** and will depend on the **direction of the price change.** For example if the average bus fare were to rise from 60p to 100p, the PED would be 0.34. The percentage change in quantity demanded is 23% while the percentage change in price is 67%. When the price fell from 100p to 60p the elasticity was 0.75.

▶ The PED for all **normal goods** will be **negative** because a rise in price will cause a fall in quantity demanded and vice versa. When, however, we analyse the significance of the PED the **sign is always ignored**.

What the elasticity figures tell us

▶ **If the PED is less than 1, the good is inelastic.** Demand is not very responsive to changes in price. In our bus example, a 40% fall in price led to a 30% rise in quantity demanded. The price elasticity was equal to 0.75.

▶ **If the PED is greater than 1, the good is price elastic.** Demand is highly responsive to a change in price. In our bus example, a 50% fall in price led to a 75% increase in quantity demanded. The price elasticity was equal to 1.5.

▶ **If the PED is equal to 1, the good has unit elasticity.** The percentage change in quantity demanded is equal to the percentage change in price. Demand changes **proportionately** with a price change. This is illustrated in Diagram 3.1 (c).

▶ **If the PED is equal to zero, the good is perfectly inelastic.** A change in price will have no influence on quantity demanded. The demand curve for such a product will be vertical. This is illustrated in Diagram 3.1 (c).

▶ **If the PED is infinity, the good is perfectly elastic.** Any change in price will see quantity demanded fall to zero. This is illustrated in Diagram 3.1 (c). The demand curve is associated with firms operating in **perfectly competitive markets** (see Chapter 6).

The diagrams for the various demand curves are illustrated below:

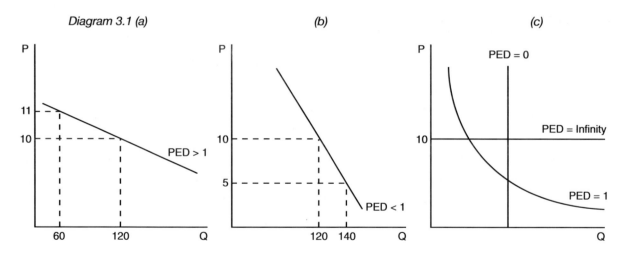

Diagram 3.1 (a)   (b)   (c)

▶ In Diagram 3.1 (a), the price rise from 10p to 11p results in a 50% fall in quantity demanded, which is greater than the 10% rise in price. The PED = 5. As this is greater than 1, the good is **elastic**.

▶ In Diagram 3.1 (b), the fall in price from 10p to 5p results in a 17% rise in quantity demanded, which is less than the 50% fall in price. The PED = 0.34. As this is less than 1, the good is **inelastic**.

FACTORS THAT DETERMINE THE VALUE OF PRICE ELASTICITY OF DEMAND

1. **Number of close substitutes within the market** – The more close substitutes available in a market, the more elastic demand will be in response to a change in price. In this case, the **substitution effect** (see Chapter 2) will be quite strong. A large rise in the price of one brand of washing powder will result in many consumers switching to one of the other brands. As a result, demand will be **elastic**. A large rise in the price of petrol will only lead to a very small fall in demand as there are no real substitutes. As a result, demand will be **inelastic**.

2. **Luxuries and necessities** – **Necessities** tend to have a more **inelastic** demand curve, whereas **luxury goods**

and services tend to be more elastic. If prices rise, most consumers will only marginally reduce their consumption of necessities, such as bread, but they are more likely to cut back on their purchases of luxuries that they do not actually need. For example, the demand for opera tickets is more elastic than the demand for urban rail travel. The demand for holiday air travel is more elastic than the demand for business air travel.

3. **Percentage of income spent on a good** – It may be the case that the smaller the proportion of income spent on a good or service, the more inelastic demand will be. A 10% rise in the price of a good costing a few pence, such as matches, is more likely to be absorbed than a 10% rise in the price in the price of good costing thousands of pounds. As a result, demand for more expensive items, which take up a large proportion of income, is likely to be more sensitive to price changes.

4. **Habit forming goods** – Goods such as cigarettes and drugs tend to be inelastic in demand. Preferences are such that habitual consumers of these products become de-sensitised to any price changes.

5. **Time period under consideration** – Demand tends to be **more elastic in the long run** rather than in the short run. For example, after the two world oil price shocks of the 1970s – the 'response' to higher oil prices was modest in the immediate period after the price increases but, as time has passed, users have found ways to consume less petroleum and other oil based products. They have purchased cars that give better mileage per gallon, spent more on insulating their homes and, more recently, started to purchase cars powered by cheaper alternatives such as liquid petroleum gas. The demand for oil has become more elastic in the long run.

PRICE ELASTICITY OF DEMAND ALONG A LINEAR DEMAND CURVE

Elasticity varies along a straight-line demand curve as illustrated in Diagram 3.2.

Diagram 3.2

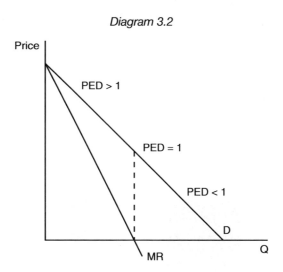

- Elasticity is not the same as slope!
- Price elasticity changes as we move along a demand curve.
- As price increases, demand becomes more elastic.
- As price falls, demand becomes more inelastic.

Demand tends to be price elastic when the marginal revenue curve (MR) is positive. Marginal Revenue is equal to the change in **total revenue** as a result of selling one extra unit of output, and is explained in Chapter 5. **At the point when MR is zero the price elasticity of demand is equal to one**. It is inelastic when marginal revenue is negative. Here, a fall in price, although causing an increase in demand, actually reduces the total revenue of producers.

USING PRICE ELASTICITY OF DEMAND

TOTAL REVENUE AND PROFIT

It is important for producers to know the PED of their output when making pricing decisions. Pricing decisions have a key impact on a firm's total revenue and profit.

▶ **Total revenue** = selling price x quantity sold.

▶ **Profit** = total revenue – total cost.

Both these concepts are explored further in Chapter 5, but price elasticity has a key impact on both variables.

▶ When a good is **price elastic** a **fall in price** will cause **a rise in total spending** on the good.

▶ When demand is **price inelastic** a **rise in price** will cause a **rise in total spending** on the good.

Diagram 3.3

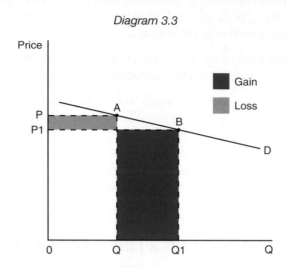

In Diagram 3.3, demand is **price elastic**. At the original price P, total revenue was equal to the area OPAQ. Following the price fall to P1, the new area of total revenue is equal to 0P1BQ1. The fall in price from P to P1 results in a rise in total revenue because **the area of gain exceeds the area of loss**.

Although there is a rise in total revenue it cannot be immediately assumed that a firm's profit will rise. This is because there is also a **rise in the firm's total costs** as output has increased from Q to Q1. In this instance the **effect on profit is therefore ambiguous** as both revenue and costs have increased. It is impossible to tell accurately whether profits will rise or fall.

Diagram 3.4

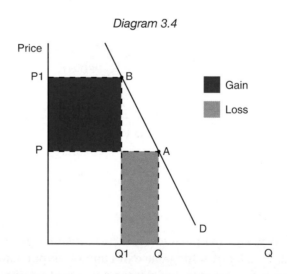

In Diagram 3.4, demand is inelastic. At the original price P, total revenue was equal to the area OPAQ. Following the price rise to P1, the new area of total revenue is equal to 0P1BQ1. The rise in price from P to P1 results in a rise in total revenue **because the area of gain exceeds the area of loss**.

The effect on profit in this case is more clear-cut because there is also a **fall in the firm's total costs** as output has decreased from Q to Q1. As the firm's revenue has increased while its costs have fallen, its **profit will rise**.

Calculating changes in demand

If a firm knows the price elasticity of demand of its output it can use this information to calculate how much demand will vary following a change in price. Suppose the PED for baked beans is (-) 0.4, it is possible to calculate exactly how much demand will fall following a rise in price.

The percentage change in demand = percentage change in price x PED.

If prices rose by 10%, then quantity demanded will fall by 4% (10% x -0.4) = -4%. This information can be used by firms for **business planning**:

▶ to estimate changes in **production levels**.

▶ to identify whether **employment** in the firm will need to change.

▶ to analyse how changes in demand will affect **stocks**.

OTHER USES OF PED

▶ What happens to the **current account** when the **exchange rate** appreciates or depreciates? See Chapter 16 for a discussion on how price elasticity of demand is used to consider the effects of exchange rate fluctuations.

▶ Why do Telecom companies charge less for their calls in the evening than they do during the day? See Chapter 6 to see how elasticity is important when firms decide to introduce **price discrimination** as a strategy to increase total revenue and profits.

▶ Will a business always pass on an indirect tax to consumers in the form of higher prices? See Chapter 4 on applications of price theory.

INCOME ELASTICITY OF DEMAND (YED)

Income elasticity of demand measures the responsiveness of demand to a change in the **real incomes** of consumers.

Income elasticity of demand (YED) $\quad = \quad \dfrac{\text{\% change in the quantity demanded of good X}}{\text{\% change in the real income of consumers}}$

NORMAL AND INFERIOR GOODS

When interpreting an income elasticity estimate, the first factor to consider is the **sign of the elasticity**. For most goods there is a positive relationship between the level of income and quantity demanded and, therefore the income elasticity will be **positive**. For example, if the income elasticity of demand for a product is +0.6 then a 20% rise in real incomes will lead to a 12% increase in demand (20% x 0.6 =12%).

If a good experiences a fall in demand when incomes rise it will have a **negative** income elasticity, and is termed as being **inferior.** For example, if the income elasticity of demand for another good is -0.3, the same 20% increase in real incomes will cause the demand for the good to fall by 6%. (20% x -0.3 = -6%).

The relationship between quantity and real income is illustrated in Diagram 3.5.

Diagram 3.5

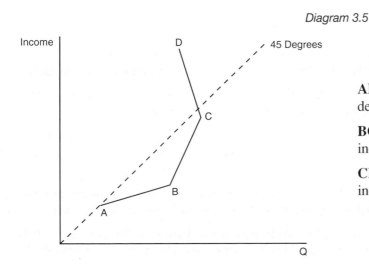

AB illustrates a YED > 1, since the change in demand is greater than the change in income.

BC illustrates a YED < 1, since the change in income is greater than the change in demand.

CD illustrates a YED < 0, since a rise in income results in a fall in demand.

13

▶ For **normal goods** (mobile phones, steak, air travel and foreign holidays) the YED is **positive**. If the YED > 1, the good is considered to be a **luxury** and the proportion of income, or **budget share,** spent on the good rises with income. If the YED < 1, the good is considered to be a **necessity** and the **budget share falls** with income.

▶ For **inferior goods** the YED is **negative**. Examples of inferior goods were given in Chapter 2.

USING INCOME ELASTICITY OF DEMAND

SHIFTS IN DEMAND

The value of an income elasticity is important to a firm as it determines the size of a **shift in demand**. Suppose a computer firm has two products, a desktop with an income elasticity of +0.5 and a laptop with an income elasticity of +3.5. If real national incomes are forecast to grow by 3% next year the firm can calculate the rise in demand for its products. Demand for desktops will rise by 1.5% (3% x +0.5 = 1.5%) and demand for laptops will increase by 10.5% (3% x +3.5 = 10.5%).

If demand for both types of computer is currently 1000 units per month, then demand for both products **will shift to the right**, as more will be demanded at each and every price. However, the **size of the shift** in demand will be different. The demand for laptops will shift further to the right than the demand for desktops. This is because demand for desktops will rise by 15 units (1,000 x 0.015 = 15) while demand for laptops will rise by 105 (1,000 x 0.105 = 105).

The firm can use the YED estimate when **planning** changes in **output, employment and stocks**. When the product, such as a laptop, has a high income elasticity of demand, such as laptops, producers should be aware that demand will be highly sensitive to the living standards of consumers. In an **economic boom**, they can expect rising sales as demand shifts to the right but, in a **recession**, they should be prepared for falling demand and a fall in their **total revenue.**

The demand for **luxury boats** is likely to be more sensitive to the **economic cycle** than the demand for **basic foods** in supermarkets.

OTHER USES OF YED

▶ **Balance of payments** – if the YED for imports exceeds the YED for exports, there are some serious implications for the economy. If the UK economy grows at the same rate as the rest of the world, demand in the UK for foreign goods and services will increase more rapidly than the world's demand for UK produced goods and services. This may cause the **current account** to worsen. This is examined in Chapter 16.

▶ **Government** – can use estimates of income elasticities to calculate the impact on demand of **income tax** cuts which boost disposable incomes. They also use YED when making calculations about projected rates of economic growth and how different sectors of the economy are likely to be affected by changing incomes.

CROSS PRICE ELASTICITY OF DEMAND (CPED)

This is defined as the **responsiveness of demand for good X following changes in the price of a related good Y.**

$$\text{Cross Price Elasticity of Demand (CPED)} = \frac{\% \text{ change in the quantity demanded of Good X}}{\% \text{ change in the price of Good Y}}$$

The main use of cross price elasticity concerns changes in the prices of **substitutes and complements.** When interpreting a cross price elasticity of demand estimate, the first factor to consider is the **sign of the elasticity**.

▶ **Substitute goods** are in competitive demand. A rise in the price of local bus travel, which is a substitute for rail travel, should cause a rise in the demand for rail travel. The **CPED will be positive.**

▶ **Complements** are goods that are in joint demand. A rise in the price of DVD players should cause a fall in demand not only for these products, but also for DVDs as the two goods are in joint demand. **The CPED will be negative.**

When examining the closeness of the relationship between two goods, we must ignore the sign of the cross price elasticity. The **higher the value of the elasticity** the **closer the relationship** between the two goods.

▶ If the CPED for two substitute goods is greater than 1, the goods are **close substitutes**. Suppose the CPED of local rail travel with respect to the price of local bus travel is +2. A 10% rise in the price of bus travel will cause a 20% rise in the demand for rail travel and, therefore, the **demand curve for rail travel will shift to the right**. If the CPED was **+0.4** (less than 1), the goods are **weak substitutes**. A 10% rise in the price of bus travel will only cause a 4% rise in the demand for rail travel, and a much smaller shift in demand.

▶ If the CPED for two complementary goods is greater than one, the goods are **close complements**. Suppose the CPED of DVDs with respect to the price of DVD players is **-1.2**. A 10% rise in the price of DVD players will cause a 12% fall in the demand for DVDs and, therefore, the **demand curve for DVDs will shift to the left**. If the CPED was **-0.2** (less than one), the goods are **weak complements**. A 10% rise in the price of DVD players will only cause a 2% fall in the demand for DVDs, and a much smaller shift in demand.

▶ If the CPED is **zero** the goods are **independent**. For example, there would be no relationship between the price of bananas and the demand for cars.

Cross price elasticity is illustrated in Diagrams 3.6 and 3.7.

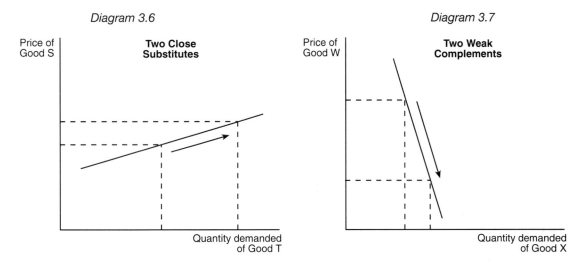

In Diagram 3.6, we see the effect of a rise in the price of Good S which is assumed to be a close substitute for Good T. The demand for T rises by far more than the increase in the price of S. In Diagram 3.7, we show the effect of a fall in the price of Good W which is taken to be only a weak complement to Good X. The demand for X does rise, but only by a small margin compared to the price change for its complement.

USING CROSS PRICE ELASTICITY OF DEMAND

The firm can use a CPED estimate when **planning** changes in **output, employment and stocks** in response to changes in the price of substitutes or complements. When the product has a close substitute, such as a brand of washing powder, producers should be aware that demand will be highly sensitive to changes in the price of competing products. A rise in the price of a rival brand will cause a large outward shift in demand.

ADVERTISING AND ELASTICITIES OF DEMAND

Persuasive advertising seeks to reinforce **consumer loyalty** for a particular brand by increasing the **perceived differentiation** between good X and substitute products. If advertising is effective, we expect to see a decrease in the **price elasticity of demand** for good X and a decrease in the **cross price elasticity of demand** for good X with respect to changes in the price of substitutes. Successful advertising might also affect consumers' perception of the good as being either a normal necessity, a luxury or an inferior product. Thus it has an impact on the **income elasticity of demand**.

PRICE ELASTICITY OF SUPPLY (PES)

This is defined as the **responsiveness of quantity supplied to a change in the good's own price**.

$$\text{PES} = \frac{\%\ \text{change in the quantity supplied of good X}}{\%\ \text{change in the price of good X}}$$

▶ **If the PES is greater than 1, the good is elastic.** Supply is highly responsive to a change in price. A straight line supply curve that is elastic will cut the price axis (see Diagram 3.8a). If the price rose from 10p to 11p, then the PES would be 4. The percentage change in quantity supplied is 40% while the percentage change in price is 10%.

▶ **If the PES is less than one, the good is inelastic.** Supply is not very responsive to changes in price. A straight line supply curve that is inelastic will cut the quantity axis (see Diagram 3.8b). If the price fell from 10p to 5p, then the PES would be 0.7. The percentage change in quantity supplied is 35% while the percentage change in price is 50%.

▶ **If the PES is equal to one, the good has unit elasticity.** The percentage change in quantity supplied is equal to the percentage change in price. Any straight line supply curve that originates from the origin has a PES of equal to one (see Diagram 3.8c).

▶ **If the PES is equal to zero, the good is perfectly inelastic.** A change in price has no effect on the quantity supplied. The supply to the market is assumed to be fixed and will not change with price (see Diagram 3.8c). A football stadium has a perfectly inelastic supply curve as the stadiums capacity cannot be changed even if there is massive demand from spectators to watch a match.

▶ **If the PES is infinity, the good is perfectly elastic.** Any change in price will see quantity supplied fall to zero (see Diagram 3.8c).

The diagrams for the various supply curves are illustrated below.

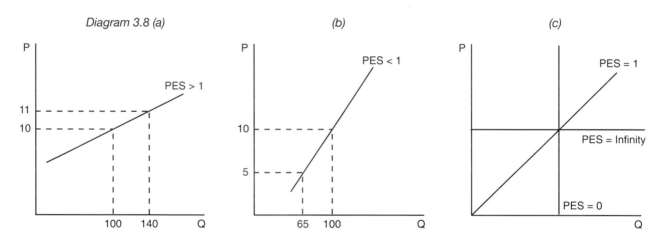

FACTORS INFLUENCING ELASTICITY OF SUPPLY

1. **Level of spare capacity** – if firms are working well below **full capacity** they can increase supply quickly and will have elastic supply curves. The higher the amount of spare capacity – the more elastic the supply. This is particularly relevant when an industry has experienced a downturn in demand leaving plenty of **under-utilised** productive resources.

2. **Substitutability of factors of production** – if factors of production can be easily moved into the production of a good or service, supply will be elastic. When demand for MP3 players increased, if resources used to make CD players were easily switched into the production of MP3 players, then supply could have responded to meet the demand.

3. **Level of stocks and work in progress** – if firms have low levels of **stocks** (or **inventories**) they may not be able to respond quickly to changes in demand and will therefore have inelastic supply curves. In contrast, when a producer has a high level of unsold stocks they can supply extra output quickly to a market (although they may have to discount prices heavily to offload excess stock). This is sometimes seen in the car industry.

4. **Time period under consideration** – in the **short run**, at least one factor is assumed to be fixed. This will tend to limit the elasticity of supply. Supply will become more elastic in the **long run** when all factor inputs in the production process can be varied and a business can alter the scale of production to meet changing demand.

5. **Production lags** – in some industries there are clearly understood **production lags** where there is an inevitable time lag between using the factor inputs and the final product becoming available. This includes agricultural markets where supply cannot always respond elastically to fluctuations in demand. In the very short run the supply of products, such as cereals, may be perfectly inelastic.

CHANGES IN EQUILIBRIUM PRICE AND OUTPUT

THE EFFECT OF A SHIFT IN DEMAND

Ceteris paribus, a shift in the demand curve to the **right**, will **raise prices** and **increase the quantity supplied**.

Diagram 4.1

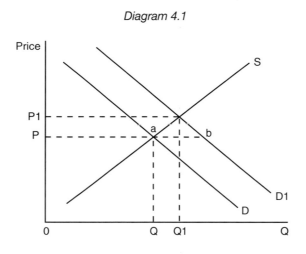

In Diagram 4.1 it is assumed that the market for a normal good is in equilibrium at price P and quantity Q. Suppose there is now an increase in **consumers' real income** that causes the demand curve to shift to the **right** from D to D1. At the **original price** P there is a **shortage** (a-b). This shortage will cause prices to be bid upwards which results in an **expansion** along the supply curve until a new equilibrium is established at a **higher price** (P1) and a **higher level of output** (Q1). The more **inelastic the supply curve, the larger** the increase in price and the **smaller** the rise in output.

When **demand shifts to the right** the firm experiences a **rise in total revenue** (price x quantity). The shaded area in Diagram 4.2 shows the increase in total revenue. At price P, the original level of total revenue is equal to 0PaQ. Following the outward shift in demand, the new level of total revenue is 0P1bQ1.

Although there is a rise in total revenue it cannot be immediately assumed that a firm's profit will rise. This is because there is also a **rise in the firm's total costs** as output has increased from Q to Q1. In this instance the **effect on profit is therefore ambiguous**, since both revenue and costs have increased. It is impossible to tell accurately whether profits will rise or fall.

Diagram 4.2

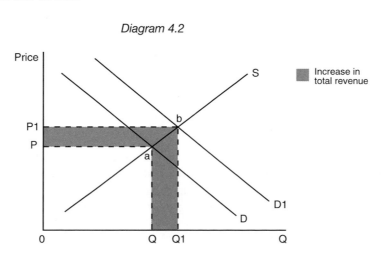

THE EFFECT OF A SHIFT IN SUPPLY

Ceteris paribus, a shift in the supply curve to the **right**, will **reduce price** and **increase quantity demanded**.

In Diagram 4.3, the market is in equilibrium at price P and quantity Q. Suppose there is now a technological advance which causes the **supply curve** to shift to the **right** from S to S1. At the **original price** P there will be a **surplus** (a-b). Suppliers will lower their prices to reduce stocks and this will result in an **expansion** along the demand curve until a new equilibrium is established at a **lower price** (P1) and a **higher level of output** (Q1). The more **inelastic** the demand curve the **larger** the fall in price and **smaller** the increase in output.

Diagram 4.3

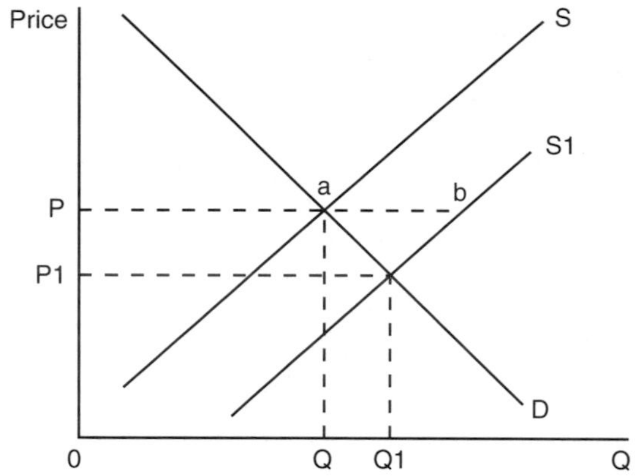

When **supply shifts to the right** the impact on total revenue depends on the price elasticity of demand. In Diagram 4.4, demand is inelastic. At the original price P, total revenue was equal to the area OPaQ. Following the outward shift in supply, the new area of total revenue is equal to 0P1bQ1. The fall in price from P to P1 results in a fall in total revenue **because the area of loss exceeds the area of gain**.

The effect on profit in this case is clear-cut, as there is also a **rise in the firm's total costs** because output has increased from Q to Q1. As the firm's revenue has decreased while its costs have increased, its **profit will fall**.

Diagram 4.4

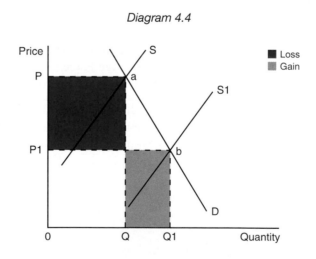

SHIFTS IN DEMAND AND SUPPLY

In Diagram 4.5 there has been an **outward shift of the supply curve** caused by a fall in input costs and an **outward shift of the demand curve** due to a successful advertising and marketing campaign. The overall effect is a large increase in the quantity traded at the new equilibrium point and a small rise in the market clearing price. This is because the size of the increase in the demand outweighs the increase in supply.

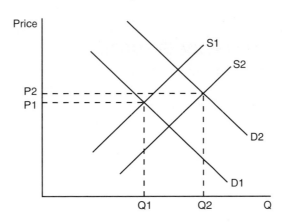

Diagram 4.5

CONSUMER SURPLUS

Consumer surplus measures the **welfare** that consumers derive from the consumption of goods and services. It is the difference between what consumers are **willing to pay** for a good or service (indicated by the position of the demand curve) and what they **actually pay** (the market price). The level of consumer surplus is shown by the **area under the demand curve and above the ruling market price** and is illustrated below in Diagram 4.6.

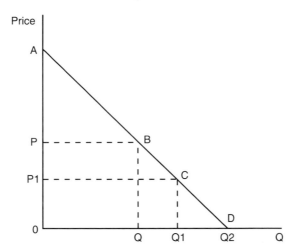

Diagram 4.6

▶ Consumer surplus = total willingness to pay for a good or service minus the total amount consumers actually do pay.

▶ Consider the demand for public transport shown in the diagram. The initial fare is price P for all passengers.

▶ At price P, the level of consumer surplus is shown by the area APB. If the bus company cuts price to P1 the new level of consumer surplus is AP1C. This means that the level of consumer welfare has increased by the area PP1CB.

▶ If a zero fare is charged, consumers will demand bus journeys up to the point where the demand curve cuts the quantity axis. Demand expands to Q2 and total consumer surplus is the entire area underneath the demand curve.

CONSUMER SURPLUS AND ELASTICITY OF DEMAND

▶ **When demand for a product is perfectly elastic,** the level of consumer surplus is **zero** since the price consumers pay exactly matches the price they are willing to pay. There must be perfect substitutes in the market for this to be the case.

► When demand is **perfectly inelastic** the amount of consumer surplus is **infinite**. Demand is invariant to a price change.

CHANGES IN DEMAND AND CONSUMER SURPLUS

When there is a shift in the demand curve leading to a change in the equilibrium price and quantity traded, the amount of consumer surplus will alter. This is shown in Diagram 4.7. Following a shift in demand from D to D1, the price rises to P1 and quantity traded expands to Q1. Consumer surplus was initially shown by the triangle AP0B. This rises to area EP1C.

Diagram 4.7

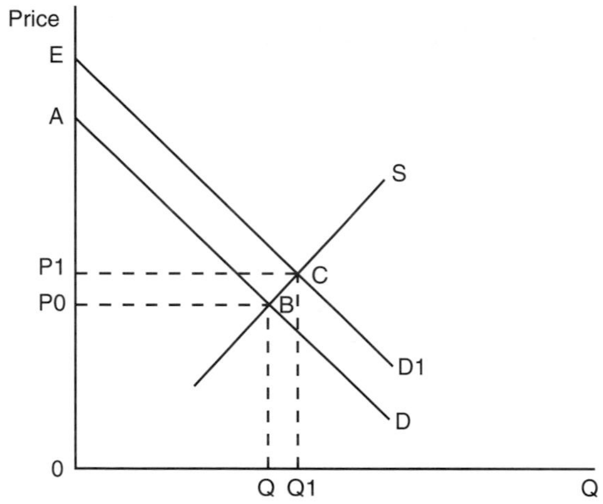

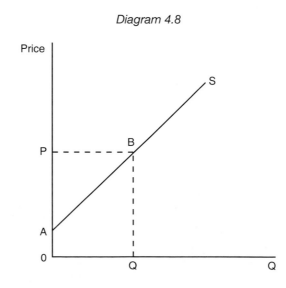

PRODUCER SURPLUS

Producer surplus is used as a measure of **producer welfare**. It is defined as being the difference between the price at which producers are willing and able to supply a good (indicated by the position of the supply curve) and the price they actually receive. The level of producer surplus is shown by the **area above the supply curve and below the market price** and is illustrated below in Diagram 4.8.

Diagram 4.8

► The minimum price that the firm needs in order to supply the good to the market is 0A. As the market price rises, supply expands (we move up the supply curve).

► At price P the level of producer surplus is represented by the area APB. This is part of the firm's total revenue which is indicated by the rectangle 0PBQ.

► The more elastic the supply curve, the smaller the amount of producer surplus. If the supply curve is

perfectly elastic, producer surplus is **zero** since the price at which the firm is willing to supply its output is also the ruling market price.

INDIRECT TAXES

Indirect taxes are a tax on expenditure imposed by the government on producers. The burden of the tax can be passed onto consumers depending on the price elasticity of demand and the price elasticity of supply for the product.

Indirect taxes raise a firm's costs and therefore cause an upward shift in the firm's supply curve. This means that less can be supplied at each price. A **unit tax** (or **specific tax**) will cause a **parallel shift** in the supply curve and is illustrated in Diagram 4.9. The vertical distance between the supply curves shows the amount of tax per unit.

An **ad valorem (percentage) tax** will cause the supply curve to **tilt to the left**. This is because the size of the tax increases with price. This is illustrated in Diagram 4.10. For example a 17.5% tax on £1 is 17.5p, much smaller than the same tax of £17.50 on £100.

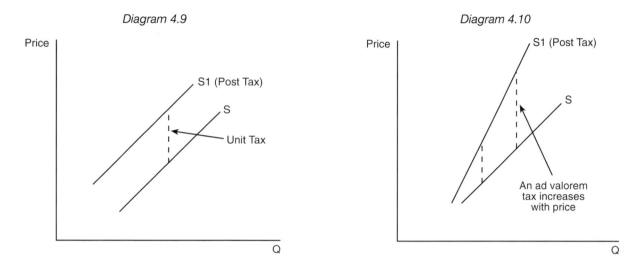

Diagram 4.9   *Diagram 4.10*

The effects of indirect taxation on consumers and producers are dependent on the price elasticity of demand.

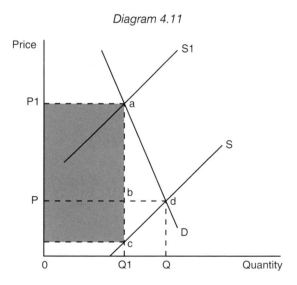

Diagram 4.11

► In Diagram 4.11 demand is **relatively price inelastic**. The producer finds it easier to pass on the tax to the consumer. The total tax per unit is ac, but the consumer pays the majority of the tax (ab) while the producer burden is bc. The quantity produced in equilibrium contracts from Q to Q1. Total tax revenue = tax per unit (ac) x quantity traded (Q1), and is represented by the shaded area.

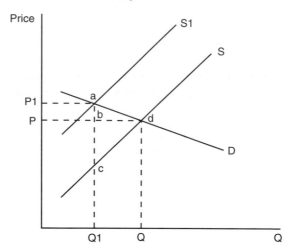

Diagram 4.12

▶ In Diagram 4.12 demand is **relatively price elastic**. The producer finds it difficult to pass on the tax to the consumer and has to **absorb** the majority of the tax itself. The producer burden (bc) outweighs the consumer burden (ab). There is a larger contraction in the quantity bought and sold – with the equilibrium quantity falling from Q to Q1.

▶ When demand is inelastic the consumer faces a large price rise and, as a result, the fall in **consumer surplus** (PP1ad) is greater than when demand is elastic.

▶ The government would rather place indirect taxes on inelastic goods and services. This is because the tax causes a relatively small fall in the quantity consumed and, as a result, the total revenue (or tax yield) from the tax will be greater. The tax yield is shown in Diagram 4.11. A series of tax increases when the demand remains inelastic will **yield** successively higher amounts of tax revenue.

The effect of indirect taxes on goods and services also depends on the degree of competition between producers in a market. In some industries, particularly those for luxury goods where the demand is relatively elastic, intense price competition between producers may limit the extent to which a firm is prepared to pass on any extra taxes to consumers.

PRODUCER SUBSIDIES

Subsidies represent payments to producers by the government, which effectively reduce costs and encourage them to increase output. The effect of a subsidy with a downward sloping demand curve is to increase the quantity of goods sold and to reduce the market equilibrium price. Government subsidies are often offered to producers of **merit goods and services** (see Chapter 7) and to industries requiring some **protection** from low cost international competition.

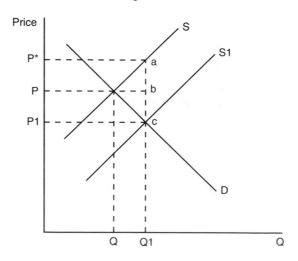

Diagram 4.13

▶ Diagram 4.13 shows a **specific subsidy** equal to ac per unit produced.

▶ The subsidy causes the firm's **supply curve** to shift to the right because the firm's costs are reduced. Equilibrium price falls from P to P1 and quantity traded expands from Q to Q1.

▶ The total amount spent by the government on the subsidy is equal to the unit subsidy (ac) x Q1. This is equal to the area P1P*ac. The consumer gain is equal to the distance (bc) while the producer gain is equal to (ab).

▶ The more inelastic the demand curve, the greater fall in prices and the greater the consumer's gain from a subsidy. Indeed when demand is perfectly inelastic the consumer gains the entire subsidy.

TARIFFS IN INTERNATIONAL MARKETS

A tariff is a tax levied on the value of imports. The factors that might explain the reasons for the implementation of protectionism are discussed in Chapter 15.

In an international market domestic consumers can purchase goods from either domestic or foreign suppliers. It is assumed in our example that an infinite number of foreign goods can be purchased at a constant world price P. This means that the world supply curve for the product is perfectly elastic at price P.

Diagram 4.14

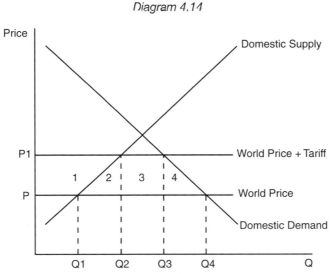

▶ In the pre-tariff situation at world price P, domestic supply is Q1 and domestic demand is Q4. The difference is met by imports (Q1-Q4). The implementation of the tariff effectively raises the world price to P1. Domestic supply expands to Q2, while demand contracts to Q3. The new post-tariff level of imports is Q2-Q3. If there is no retaliation by other countries, this fall in imports may reduce a current account deficit (see Chapter 16).

▶ The rise in price reduces the level of consumer surplus by the Area 1+2+3+4. Although consumer welfare has been reduced, producers and the government both gain from the tariff.

▶ Producer surplus has increased by Area 1. The expansion in domestic output means that producers also receive Area 2 in the form of higher revenue. The expansion in domestic output may also lead to a rise in employment.

▶ The government receives revenue from the tariff equal to Area 3. This is calculated by multiplying the tariff by the level of imports Q2-Q3.

▶ Part of the fall in consumer surplus is not redistributed to any economic agent. Area 4 represents the deadweight welfare cost of the tariff.

▶ The effectiveness of a tariff in reducing the level of imports is determined by the elasticity of demand and supply. The more elastic the demand and supply curves, the greater the fall in imports will be following the implementation of a tariff.

GOVERNMENT INTERVENTION – MAXIMUM AND MINIMUM PRICES

MAXIMUM PRICES

Governments can impose legally binding **maximum prices** to set a statutory **price ceiling** in a market. To be effective a maximum price must be set *below* the free market price. In Diagram 4.15 the normal free market equilibrium is P0. The government then imposes a maximum price of P1.

Diagram 4.15

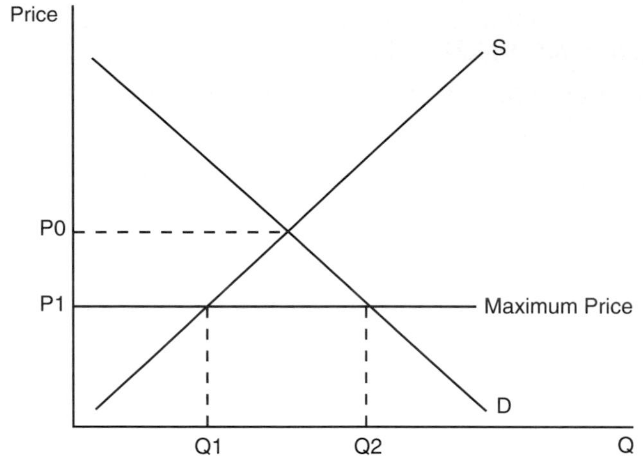

Price

P0

P1 —————————————————————— Maximum Price

Q1   Q2   Q

- ▶ Because the price ceiling is P1, there will be a contraction of market supply and expansion of market demand leading to a **shortage** in the market equal to Q1-Q2.

- ▶ This shortage could lead to the development of a **black market** since the price ceiling is below the free market level. In order to assure a fair distribution of the product the government may also introduce **rationing**.

MINIMUM PRICES

A minimum price is a **price floor** below which the free market price cannot fall. A good example of this is **minimum wage legislation** which is illustrated in Diagram 4.16. To be effective the minimum price has to be set above the normal equilibrium price.

Diagram 4.16

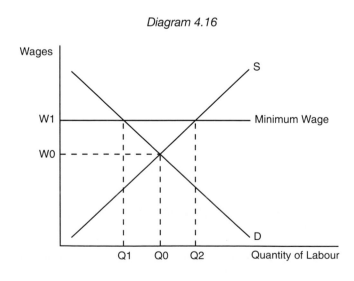

- ▶ Consider the market for low-skilled labour shown in the diagram. The normal free market wage would be established at W0.

- ▶ If the minimum wage is set at W1, there will be an excess supply of labour equal to Q2-Q1. This is because the demand for labour contracts, whilst the supply of labour willing to work at this wage rate expands.

▶ The result will be unemployment in the labour market. While the minimum wage may raise earnings for those in employment, it clearly has a negative impact on the level of unemployment.

MAXIMUM AND MINIMUM PRICING POLICIES

Agricultural products often experience volatile price changes because both demand and supply are inelastic in the short-run. Shifts in both can therefore cause large fluctuations in the equilibrium price. This price volatility can have a damaging effect on producer incomes, employment and capital investment spending in agriculture.

In agricultural markets the government uses **buffer stocks** and other forms of **intervention** to keep prices within a fixed band. If the price is falling towards its floor, the government will purchase a quantity of the commodity and add it to its stockpile. Conversely, when the price is rising towards its ceiling the government will sell some of its stockpile on the open market. In this way supply and demand are manipulated to keep price within its specified range.

Intervention in markets to affect the price level is not limited solely to agricultural markets. The government might also wish to change the **exchange rate** and can intervene in the Foreign Exchange Markets to change the value of the currency (see Chapter 17).

When entrepreneurs combine the factors of production to produce output there will undoubtedly be costs involved. This Chapter only considers the private costs to firms. Costs to other members of society that firms do not consider when producing their output, such as pollution, are examined in greater detail in Chapter 7.

In economics there are **two time periods,** the short run and the long run:

▶ The **short run** is a period of time when there is **at least one fixed factor of production.** This means that at least one of the factors of production discussed in Chapter 1 cannot be altered, and this is usually land and/or capital. Output can only be increased when additional units of **variable factors** (labour, raw materials) are added to the fixed factors.

▶ In the **long run, all factors of production are variable**. A business can change the whole scale of production by varying all the factors of production. This means all inputs into the production process can be varied.

It is impossible to put an actual period of time on the short run. A market trader may be able to buy a new stall and hire a new pitch in a day, whereas for a firm producing nuclear power it could take a decade to build a new power station.

SHORT RUN COSTS

In order to understand short run costs it is essential to understand the **productivity** of the variable factor and the **law of diminishing returns.** In most examples, labour is assumed to be the only factor that can be varied in the short run. The **returns to labour** are usually measured by **marginal product**:

Marginal product (MP) = the change in total output resulting from adding one extra unit of labour.

The **law of diminishing returns** states that as we add more units of the variable factor (labour) to fixed amounts of land and capital the change in total output will first rise and then fall.

Diminishing returns to labour occurs when **marginal product** starts to fall. This means that total output will increase at a decreasing rate when more workers are employed.

WHY WILL MARGINAL PRODUCT FIRST RISE THEN FALL?

The behaviour of marginal product is linked directly to the **productivity** of each additional worker. At low levels of employment the fixed factors of production, land and capital are **underutilised.** This means that each additional worker will be have plenty of capital to use and, as a result, **marginal product** will rise. However, beyond a certain point, the fixed factors of production become scarcer and new workers will not have any capital with which to work. Indeed, eventually the workers will start to get in each other's way. As a result, the productivity of each additional worker falls.

The implications of the law of diminishing returns on short run costs can now be examined.

KEY SHORT RUN COSTS
TOTAL COSTS (TC) = TOTAL FIXED COST (TFC) + TOTAL VARIABLE COSTS (TVC)

1. FIXED COSTS

These costs relate to the fixed factors of production and **do not vary directly with the level of output.**

Examples include:
• rent
• the leasing costs of equipment
• business rates
• salaried staff

- interest repayments on loans
- depreciation of capital (due to age)
- insurance
- advertising expenditure

All these costs are classed as total fixed costs (TFC) because they would still have to be paid even if the firm produced no output. Indeed, they remain **constant even as output increases.**

Average fixed cost (AFC) = $\dfrac{\text{Total Fixed Costs (TFC)}}{\text{Output (Q)}}$

Average fixed costs will **fall continuously** as output rises. This is because the total fixed costs are being spread over a higher level of production causing the average cost to fall.

2. VARIABLE COSTS

These are costs that **vary directly with output** since additional units of the variable factors are required to increase output. Examples include:

- raw materials and component costs
- wages of manufacturing staff
- electricity and gas costs
- depreciation of capital inputs due to wear and tear
- transport costs

There are some costs that are difficult to categorise as either fixed or variable. Labour costs that are related to the production of output are classed as variable whereas staffing costs that relate to administration or management are classed as fixed. This is because these costs do not vary with the level of output. The distinction, however, is not clear cut. Some economists would describe an electricity bill as **semi-fixed** as there is a fixed standing charge as well as a variable part of the bill based on consumption.

Average variable cost (AVC) = $\dfrac{\text{Total Variable Costs (TVC)}}{\text{Output (Q)}}$

The shape of the AVC is strongly influenced by productivity of labour, if we assume additional units of labour can be hired at a constant cost. As productivity (output per worker) starts to decline there will be upward pressure on average variable costs.

Average total cost (ATC) = $\dfrac{\text{Total Cost (TC)}}{\text{Output (Q)}}$

MARGINAL COSTS

These are defined as the change in total costs resulting from increasing output by one unit. Marginal costs relate to variable costs only. Changes in fixed costs in the short run affect total costs, but not marginal costs.

Consider the following cost schedule for a firm:

Output	Fixed Costs £	Variable Costs £	Total Costs £	Marginal Costs £
0	100	0	100	–
10	100	50	150	5
20	100	90	190	4
30	100	135	235	4.5

▶ The fixed costs do not vary with output.

▶ Total costs are calculated by adding together fixed costs and variable costs. The total costs at 10 units of output equal £100 + £50 = £150.

▶ The marginal cost of moving from zero to ten units of output is calculated by dividing the change in total costs by the change in output. The change in total costs is £50 (£150 – £100) divided by the change in output 10 units, and the marginal cost is therefore £5.

▶ The **marginal cost** of an extra unit is linked with the **marginal productivity of labour**. If marginal product is falling, assuming the cost of employing extra units of labour is constant, then the extra costs of the additional units of output will rise.

A summary of the key short run cost curves for a typical firm is shown in Diagram 5.1.

Diagram 5.1

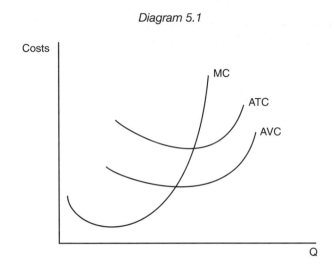

▶ It is important to note that the marginal cost curve cuts both the AVC and ATC curves at their minimum points. This can be explained in a similar way to a cricketer's batting average. If a batsman's average is 50 and he scores 60 in his next (marginal) innings his average will rise. If he scored only forty in his next (marginal) innings then his average would fall. In a similar way, when marginal cost is below the average variable cost, the average will fall. When marginal cost is above the average variable cost, the average will rise. The same analysis applies for ATC and, as a result, marginal cost will always cut the average variable and total cost curves at their minimum points.

▶ Both AVC and AFC influence the behaviour of ATC. ATC will start to rise after the rise in AVC because of the downward pressure applied by AFC. Thus ATC will only rise when the increase in AVC offsets the decline in AFC.

LONG RUN PRODUCTION AND COSTS

In the long run, all factors of production are variable. When a firm increases output it can increase all the factors of production (land labour and capital). How output responds to a change in factor inputs is called **returns to scale**.

Returns to scale in the long run

▶ **Increasing returns** to scale occur when the % change in output > % change in inputs

▶ **Decreasing returns** to scale occur when the % change in output < % change in inputs

▶ **Constant returns** to scale occur when the % change in output = % change in inputs

Returns to scale have an important influence on the shape of a firm's long run average cost curve.

LONG RUN AVERAGE COSTS

In the long run, the **scale of production** can be increased, or reduced, as all factors are variable. This allows the firm to move on to new average cost curves. For each size of firm there is an equivalent short run average cost curve. As the firm expands its output it moves on to different short run average cost curves. In this example, it would move from AC1 to AC2 to AC3. If expanding the scale of output leads to a lower average cost for each level of output, then the firm is said to be experiencing **economies of scale**. This is illustrated in Diagram 5.2.

Diagram 5.2

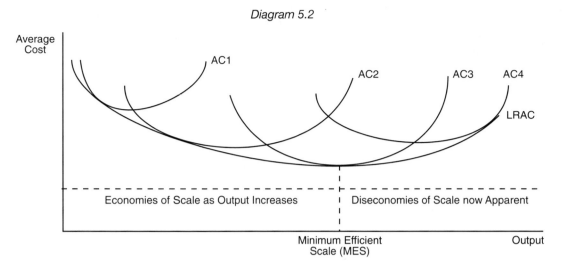

The LRAC curve is drawn on the assumption of infinite plant sizes. The points of tangency do not occur at the minimum points of the SRAC curves except at the point where the **minimum efficient scale** (MES) is achieved. This is the minimum level of output required to **exploit fully economies of scale**.

▶ If LRAC is falling when output is increasing, then the firm is said to be experiencing **economies of scale**. A doubling of inputs leads to a more than doubling of outputs and the firm is encountering **increasing returns to scale**.

▶ When LRAC starts to rise, then the firm is said to be experiencing **diseconomies of scale**. A doubling of inputs leads to a less than doubling of output and the firm is encountering **decreasing returns to scale**.

▶ If LRAC is constant, then the firm is experiencing **constant returns to scale**.

ECONOMIES OF SCALE

Internal economies of scale arise from the growth in the size of the firm itself. Good basic examples include:

▶ **Technical economies** – larger firms can employ and combine **specialist machinery** that should reduce the average costs of production. It may not be economically viable for smaller firms to purchase equipment that is highly productive because their output levels are too low to spread the cost of such machines. For example, a large supermarket could install bar code technology that will reduce the average cost of recording and ordering stock. It would not, however, be economically viable for a small corner shop to buy this technology.

Within larger firms there is also greater scope for the **specialisation of labour**. This is where the production process is split into many separate tasks allowing individual workers to become more proficient in their roles. The production line in many car plants is a good example of this concept. The increased productivity of the workforce will reduce average costs.

Another technical economy relates to the **law of increased dimensions.** This is linked to the cubic law where, for example, doubling the height and width of a tanker or building can lead to a more than proportionate increase in the cubic capacity. Examples of industries where this is important include:

- Food Retailing
- Hotels
- Motor manufacturing
- Oil & Gas distribution
- Transatlantic Airlines
- Transportation
- Warehousing/Storage

- **Marketing economies** – as a firm grows in size it can spread its advertising budget over a larger output, but most importantly it can purchase its factor inputs in bulk at negotiated discounted prices. This is particularly the case when a firm has **monopsony (buying) power** in a market. The UK supermarket sector has exploited its position as the main buyer of produce from UK farmers and, as a result, has reduced the prices it pays for fresh foodstuffs.

- **Managerial economies** – larger manufacturers can employ specialists to manage and supervise production, thus cutting managerial costs per unit. For example, larger supermarkets can afford to employ specialist buyers who can reduce their buying costs significantly. Better management and the use of specialist administrative equipment, such as networked computers that improve communication, will raise labour productivity and reduce average costs.

- **Financial economies** – larger firms are normally perceived to be more creditworthy and therefore have greater access to credit facilities, with favourable rates of borrowing. Smaller firms often face much higher rates of interest on overdrafts and loans.

External economies of scale arise from the growth in the size of the **industry**. Firms within the industry will experience a fall in long run average costs, particularly if the firms are clustered in one geographical region. The fall in average costs is caused by a number of factors:

- Firms in the industry may be able to **share the research and development** costs of new products and, as a result, their unit costs will be decreased.

- Educational establishments may set up vocational courses for students and this will **reduce the training costs** of firms. Some firms may also be able to poach trained staff from other companies in the industry.

- Component suppliers for the industry may start to set up in business. If these firms specialise in the production of supplies for the industry they may be able to attain internal economies of scale which will **reduce the unit cost of components** for the industry. Component suppliers will certainly be able to produce parts at a cheaper cost than if individual firms tried to make them themselves.

DISECONOMIES OF SCALE

Internal diseconomies of scale occur when a firm grows beyond the scale of production that minimises long-run average cost. The rise in LRAC is caused by **diseconomies of scale**. To summarise, the potential diseconomies of scale a firm may experience relate to:

- **Control** – monitoring how productive each worker is in a modern corporation is both imperfect and costly.

- **Co-ordination** – it is difficult to co-ordinate complicated production processes and they may break down. Achieving efficient flows of information in large businesses is expensive.

- **Co-operation** – workers in large firms may feel a sense of alienation. If they do not consider themselves to be an integral part of the business their productivity may fall.

External diseconomies of scale occur when the industry becomes too large forcing up long run average costs. Good examples include:

- **Higher transportation costs** caused by congestion. If an industry, clustered in one geographical region, becomes too large the surrounding roads may become congested leading to a sharp rise in distribution costs.

- **Higher raw material costs** – if an industry grows rapidly, demand for raw materials will rise which may force up prices. This will increase all firms' production costs.

INCREASING RETURNS

Much of the new thinking in business economics focuses on **increasing returns** to a company growing in size. If a business can sell more output, it may become progressively easier to sell even more output and reap the benefits of large-scale production. An excellent example of this is the computer software business. The costs of developing new software programs is very high but the marginal cost of producing extra copies of the software may be close to zero. If a company can establish itself by providing a particular piece of software, positive feedback from consumers will expand the customer base and encourage the firm to increase production. Because the marginal cost of production is so low, the extra output reduces the average costs of the business. This explains why a few large companies dominate the software market.

Why can small firms survive?

The benefits to firms of economies of scale seem enormous. Why then can any small firms remain in business? The answer is that in some industries economies of scale are not very important. This particularly applies to industries that produce made to order products where each item will be different. As a result, there will be little scope for specialisation and it is likely that one craftsman will be responsible for the whole production process. Firms like this usually offer a highly personalised service spending a great deal of time with each customer, which is something a larger firm simply could not offer. Good examples of this are specialist sports car manufacturers who produce cars to order.

NATURAL MONOPOLIES

The extent to which economies of scale can be exploited in the long-run will vary between different industries. In some the minimum efficient scale (MES) is reached at a relatively low level of output. The scale economies are limited and there is room for many separate businesses to achieve the MES. In a **natural monopoly** the cost structure is different. In industries where massive networks or distribution channels are required, the overhead costs in relation to the running costs are likely to be very high. There is also likely to be great potential to exploit technical economies of scale. As a result the MES may be a high proportion of total market demand. We assume for a natural monopoly that the long-run average cost curve falls continuously over a very large range of output. This is shown in Diagram 5.3 below.

Diagram 5.3

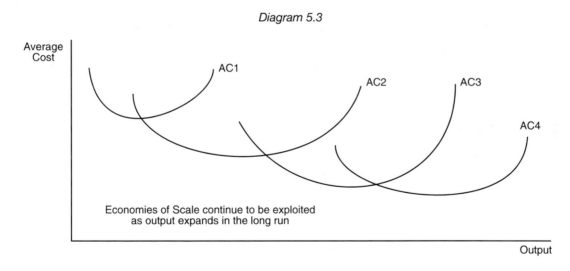

REVENUES

Revenue is simply the income generated from the sale of output in goods markets. It is also known as **turnover.**

TOTAL REVENUE = Price x Quantity

$$\textbf{AVERAGE REVENUE = PRICE} = \frac{\text{Total revenue}}{\text{Output}}$$

MARGINAL REVENUE = the change in **total revenue** as a result of selling one extra unit of output.

The Diagrams 5.4 and 5.5 below illustrate two different revenue curves.

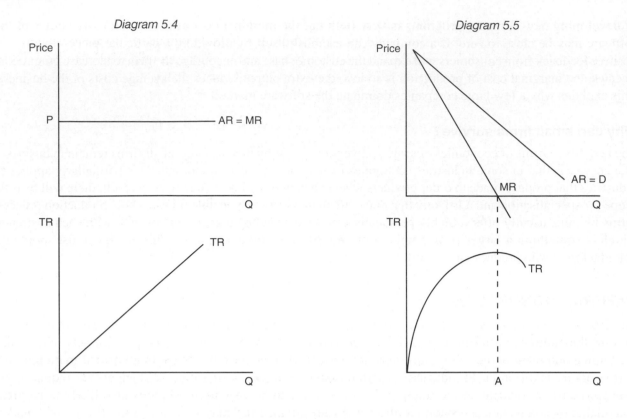

Diagram 5.4

Diagram 5.5

In Diagram 5.4 the demand curve facing the firm is perfectly elastic. As the firm sells each additional unit at a constant price AR must equal MR. The total revenue curve is a straight line because marginal revenue is both positive and constant.

In Diagram 5.5 the firm faces a downward sloping demand curve. **The MR curve is always twice the slope of the AR curve**. Total revenue is maximised when MR is zero and the elasticity of demand is equal to 1. Up to point A, MR is positive so any increases in output result in a rise in total revenue. Beyond this point MR is negative and any rise in output causes a fall in total revenue.

PROFITS AND PROFIT MAXIMISATION

▶ Profit is equal to the difference between the total revenue and total cost.

▶ Profit per unit = AR – ATC.

▶ A firm adds to profits if the marginal revenue from selling an extra unit is greater than the marginal cost of production.

Diagram 5.6

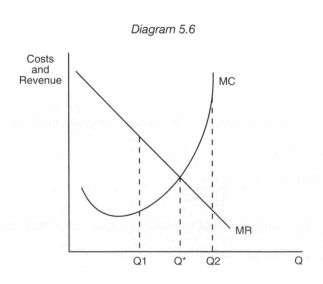

Profit maximisation occurs when MC = MR. The explanation of this is examined in Diagram 5.6. At output level Q1, MR exceeds MC and the firm could increase profit by increasing output by one additional unit. At output level Q2, MC exceeds MR and the firm could reduce its loss by reducing output by one unit. If these two statements are correct then the profit maximising rule MC = MR must be true.

In economics, there is no unique definition of profit.

Normal Profits – are defined as the minimum level of profit required to keep the factors of production in their current use in the long run. Normal profits are included in the ATC curve, thus if the firm covers its ATC it is making normal profits. Normal profit is more widely known as the **break-even point** and occurs when Price (AR) = ATC.

Abnormal Profit – is any profit in excess of normal profit and occurs when total revenue exceeds total costs, or price (AR) > ATC. It is also known as **supernormal profit**. When firms are enjoying abnormal profits in an industry there is an incentive for other producers to enter the industry to try to acquire some of this profit for themselves.

Sub-Normal Profit – is any profit less than normal profit and occurs when total revenue is less than total costs, or price (AR) < ATC.

ALTERNATIVES TO PROFIT MAXIMISATION

All the market structures examined in Chapter 6 assume that firms will maximise profits. In reality this is not always the case. It is very difficult for firms to identify their profit maximising output, as they can not accurately calculate marginal revenue and marginal costs. There may also be some very good reasons why managers may wish to pursue alternative objectives. Some of these are explained below:

Revenue maximisation – some firms may wish to increase their market share in an industry and grow in size. This may allow them to attain **economies of scale** or to gain some form of **monopoly power**. This objective may also be **driven by the management** of the company whose salaries may be linked to the size of the firm in relation to others in the industry or its sales revenue. Revenue maximisation occurs when MR is equal to zero and is shown in Diagram 5.7, at output Q2. The profit maximising level of output is Q1, and by expanding output to Q2 the firm is **reducing its profit**, but **increasing its sales revenue**. At Q2 the firms is still making an abnormal profit, as price (AR) is greater than average cost.

Sales maximisation – a firm would maximise its total sales and break even at Q3. This is where price (AR) = ATC. At this point total revenue equals total cost. If a firm expanded output any further it would make a loss and would go out of business in the long run. This objective may be driven by the same factors as revenue maximisation, but shareholders in larger business may be concerned as the firm is making no profit. This may lead to the replacement of the management.

Diagram 5.7

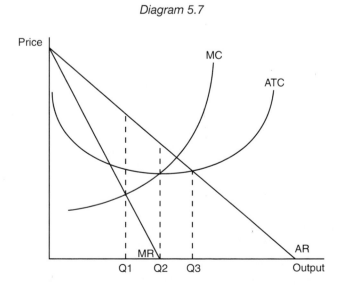

Firms may not profit maximise for other reasons:

Limit Pricing – firms may adopt predatory pricing policies by lowering prices to a level that would force any new firms entering the industry to operate at a loss. This would allow firms to sustain a monopoly position in a market.

Satisficing – this occurs when a firm does not maximise profits to keep other stakeholders in the economy satisfied. A firm may be under pressure to reduce prices to consumers if it has made large profits and may choose to do this in order to stop an investigation by the Competition Commission, or to improve its image with customers. Alternatively, the firm may reward workers with higher wages in order to stop industrial action.

THE CONCEPT OF ECONOMIC EFFICIENCY

Before being able to analyse the relative merits of different market structures it is essential to have an understanding of **economic efficiency**. Economic efficiency is closely linked to the important concept of **economic welfare**. It looks at questions such as are goods and services produced at minimum cost using scarce resources optimally? Do the prices firms charge to consumers reflect the true costs of production for each unit of output?

Allocative efficiency

In simple terms, allocative efficiency is achieved when **resources are allocated** in such a way that the **needs and wants of consumers are satisfied**. For this to happen the value consumers place on a good or service (reflected in the price they are willing to pay) must equal the cost of the resources used up in providing the product. Thus, the condition required is that **price = marginal cost (or P = MC)**.

▶ If the price > marginal cost, the firm is extracting a price from consumers that is above the cost of resources used in making the product. The result is that the product is likely to be **under-consumed**. In Diagram 6.1(a), allocative efficiency is at output Qe. This is in contrast to the profit maximising point. Where MC = MR, and price is at P1, there is **allocative inefficiency** as price is above marginal cost the good will be under-consumed.

▶ When price < marginal cost, the price paid by consumers will be less than the value of resources used in making the product. The result is that the product will be **over-consumed**.

Allocative efficiency is often confused with the concept of **Pareto Optimality**. Here, economic welfare is maximised when it is impossible to make someone else better off without making someone else worse off.

This concept was discussed in Chapter 1 and can be linked to production possibility frontiers.

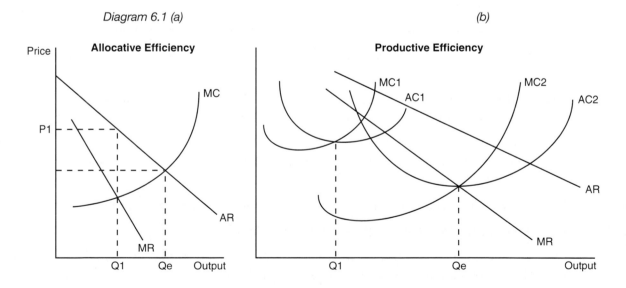

Diagram 6.1 (a)   *(b)*

Productive efficiency refers to a firm's costs of production and can be applied both to the short and long run. It is achieved when the output is produced at the minimum average total cost (AC). In the short run the firm is operating on cost curves AC1 and MC1 and the efficient output is Q1. In the long run the firm experiences some **economies of scale** and moves onto cost curves AC2 and MC2. The efficient output occurs when all the potential scale economies have been utilised at output Qe. This is also known as the **minimum efficient scale** (MES).

If productive efficiency is achieved then a firm will use the least amount of scarce resources to produce a given level of output. To be operating on the economy's production possibility frontier, all firms must be productively efficient. This is explained further in Chapter 1.

Dynamic efficiency occurs when firms are responsive to the needs and wants of consumers. For example, some economists have argued that greater competition in the airline sector has led to improvements in the quality of on-flight food and other developments, such as entertainment systems in the back of seats.

THE SPECTRUM OF COMPETITION

Market structures can be categorised by the number of suppliers there are in an industry. At one end of the spectrum are highly **competitive markets**, where **many firms** compete fiercely with each other and have no real control over the price in the market. At the other end of the spectrum is a **monopoly**. This is where there is just one firm in the market, a **sole supplier**, who can set prices. There are other types of market structure that lie between these two extremes, with **oligopoly** being one of the most common. This occurs when a **few large producers** dominate the majority of the market.

CHARACTERISTICS OF MARKET STRUCTURES

In most AS courses, students are only required to know the characteristics of each market structure. A more detailed understanding of the diagrams and economic efficiency, however, is required at A2.

PERFECT COMPETITION

A **perfectly competitive industry** is highly unlikely to exist in its entirety given the strong assumptions made about the operation of the market. We do, though, see elements of perfect competition in certain markets such as those for agricultural products and other primary commodities. These are the only markets where there are enough sellers of products that are near perfect substitutes for each other.

Main assumptions

▶ There are many sellers and, as a result, each firm produces only a small percentage of total market output. It therefore exercises **no control over the market price.** For example, it cannot restrict output in the hope of forcing up the existing market price.

▶ No individual buyer has any control over the market. i.e. there is **no monopsony power**.

▶ It follows from these two assumptions that buyers and sellers must regard the market price as beyond their control.

▶ There is **perfect freedom of entry and exit** from the industry. Firms face few or **no sunk costs** that might impede movement in and out of the market. This ensures all firms only make normal profits in the long run.

▶ Firms in the market produce **homogeneous products** that are perfect substitutes for each other. This leads to each firm being a **price taker** in the market and facing a **perfectly elastic demand curve** (average revenue curve) for their product.

▶ **Perfect knowledge** – consumers have perfect information about firms' prices and products.

▶ There are **no externalities** arising from production or consumption.

Although perfect competition may not exist in the real world, there are still markets that can be considered to be **highly competitive**. Good examples of **competitive markets** include:

- Book retailing
- Clothing
- Computer Hardware
- Home and car insurance
- Opticians
- Parcel delivery

Such markets are likely to exhibit the following features:

▶ **Low prices** because of the large number of competing firms. This will mean firms face **elastic demand** curves, and any rise in price will lead to a large fall in demand and total revenue.

▶ **Low barriers to entry** – new firms will find it easy to enter markets if they feel there is sufficient abnormal profit to be made. The entry of new firms provides extra competition and ensures prices are kept low.

▶ **Lower profits** than those in markets dominated by a few firms.

▶ **Economic efficiency** – competition will ensure that firms attempt to minimise their costs and move towards **productive efficiency**. The threat of competition should lead to a faster rate of technological diffusion, as firms have to be responsive to the needs of consumers. This is known as **dynamic efficiency.**

MONOPOLISTIC COMPETITION

In this market structure the assumptions are the same as perfect competition with one crucial exception. Firms produce **differentiated rather than homogeneous products**. This gives individual firms some ability to set prices, although the markets will still be highly competitive.

There are a number of markets that closely resemble the assumptions of monopolistic competition. Perhaps the two best examples in any town are **hairdressing** and **take-away food**.

▶ Each market has **many sellers** – they produce **differentiated products** that are not perfect substitutes for each other. For example, there are many different hairdressers in a town offering a wide range of cuts and services. In the fast food market, there are various types of food that can ordered (Indian, Chinese, pizza, fish and chips, etc.) and the quality of the food and service can vary. Many take-away firms now offer home delivery to differentiate their products.

▶ There is **freedom of entry and exit**. It is easy for firms to enter and leave the market, as there are few barriers to entry and exit. In fast food, only a basic food hygiene certificate is required to enter the market and the set-up costs are relatively small. In theory, if there is perfect freedom of entry and exit, firms will only be able to make **normal profits in the long run.**

▶ However, this assumption is unrealistic and most firms will make some abnormal profit in the long run. The profit will be small though, as the high level of competition ensures that most of the abnormal profit is competed away.

▶ In local communities, there is **good information** about the prices and quality of take-aways and hairdressers. Information can be obtained from the local press and from advertising leaflets. If one firm raises its prices it will lose demand as consumers switch to other competing firms. It will not, however, see its demand fall to zero as in perfect competition, because the products are differentiated.

These assumptions ensure that the market is **highly competitive** and, as a result, firms will face elastic demand curves. Monopolistic markets are usually very competitive and will have features very similar to those described for competitive markets in the section above.

PURE MONOPOLY

A pure monopolist is defined as a **single seller** of a product in a given market. In simple terms, this means that the firm has a **market share** of 100%. The working definition of a monopolistic market relates to any firm with greater than 25% of the industry's total sales. Monopolies can develop in a variety of ways:

▶ *Horizontal integration*
Where two firms join at the same stage of production in the same industry. For example two car manufacturers merge, or a leading bank successfully takes over another bank.

▶ *Vertical integration*
Where a firm develops market power by integrating with the different stages of production in an industry e.g. by buying its suppliers or controlling the main retail outlets. A good example is the oil industry where many of the leading companies are both producers and refiners of crude oil.

► *Creation of a statutory monopoly*
Some key industries are given monopoly status. For example, the Post Office has a legal monopoly for the delivery of letters on the UK mainland.

► *Franchises and Licences*
These give a firm the right to operate in a market – and are usually open to renewal every few years. Examples include:
- Commercial radio licences
- Commercial television
- Local taxi route licences
- Regional rail services
- The National Lottery

► *Internal expansion of a firm*
Firms can generate higher sales and increase market share by expanding their operations and exploiting possible economies of scale.

For a pure monopolist **the firm is the industry.** The firm has some power over setting price **or** output but not both. The firm is constrained by the position of its demand curve. A monopolist will usually **profit maximise** and make **large abnormal profits** in both the short and the long run. For **abnormal profits** to be maintained the existing monopolist must prevent the entry of new firms/products. This can be done through **barriers to entry**. These are the mechanisms by which **potential competitors** are blocked. Monopolies can then enjoy **high profits** in the **long run** because rival firms have not diluted their market share.

BARRIERS TO ENTRY

Barriers to entry can exist for a variety of reasons.

► *Patents*
These give a firm the legal protection to produce a patented product for a number of years. Patents are government enforced intellectual property rights to prevent the entry of rivals. They are generally assigned for 17-20 years and give the owner an exclusive right to prevent others from using their products, ideas, inventions or processes. A good example of this is the patent on the Dyson vacuum cleaner.

► *Vertical Integration*
Control over supplies and distribution can be very important. For example, many major international oil companies are fully vertically integrated. They control oil extraction, refining and retail outlets to maintain their market power.

► *Limit Pricing*
Firms may adopt predatory pricing policies by lowering prices to a level that would force any new entrants to operate at a loss.

► *Absolute cost advantages*
Lower costs, perhaps due to being in the market for some time, allow the existing monopolist to cut prices and win price wars.

► *Advertising*
High levels of advertising enable firms to establish branded products and win customer loyalty. New entrants into the market must therefore spend substantial amounts on advertising to compete, which could deter entry.

► *Sunk Costs*
Some industries have very high start-up costs or a high ratio of fixed to variable costs. Some of these costs might be unrecoverable if an entrant opts to leave the market. This acts as a disincentive to enter the industry.

► *International trade restrictions*
Trade restrictions such as tariffs and quotas should also be considered as a barrier. Foreign rivals cannot compete with firms in a protected domestic market.

KEY FEATURES OF MONOPOLY

A monopoly will generally lead to:

- **Higher prices** and **lower output**.
- **Abnormal profits** in the long run.
- **Low level of economic efficiency** with productive and allocative efficiency not being achieved.
- A **fall in consumer welfare** as consumer surplus is decreased.
- **Limited choice** for consumers.

OLIGOPOLY

An oligopoly is defined as a market **dominated by a few producers**; each of whom has some control over the market.

Examples of oligopolistic markets include:

- Electricity generation
- Petrol retailing and production
- Telecommunications
- the main UK commercial banks
- the travel industry
- the washing powder market

There is no single theory of how firms determine price and output under conditions of oligopoly, but the industry is likely to exhibit the following features:

- A few firms selling similar products.
- Each firm has branded products.
- There will be significant entry barriers into the market in the long run.
- Firms have to take into account the likely reactions of rivals when considering price changes.
- Non-price competition, in the form of promotions and special offers.

Some of the best examples of non-price competition have been recently introduced in the food retail sector:

- Traditional advertising/marketing
- Banking and other Financial Services
- Home delivery systems
- Extension of opening hours (24 hour shopping)
- Incentives to shop at off-peak times
- Loyalty cards
- In-store chemists/post offices/crèches
- Discounted petrol
- Innovative use of technology for shoppers
- Internet shopping

A key feature of oligopolistic markets is the **interdependence** of price and output decisions. Firms have to consider the likely reaction of their rivals to their own pricing strategies. This leads to **uncertainty** within the market.

Some industries may operate like monopolies with **high prices** and low levels of economic efficiency. This problem will be particularly acute if firms in an industry **collude** together and behave like a monopolist. When this happens the existing firms decide to engage in **price fixing agreements or cartels.** The aim of this is to **maximise joint profits** and act as if the market was a pure monopoly. This behaviour is illegal, but it is hard to prove that a group of firms have deliberately joined together to raise prices. In such markets consumer welfare and economic efficiency will be very low.

Other industries may, however, behave like a highly competitive market. Firms may sacrifice profits in the short run and attempt to maximise market share in the long run. This will result in fierce price competition, lower prices and high levels of consumer welfare. Recent price wars in markets include:

- Supermarkets
- Low cost airlines
- Mobile Phones
- Personal Computers
- Newspapers
- Mortgage Finance Markets

Another type of oligopolistic behaviour that occurs **is price leadership.** This is when one firm has a **dominant position** in the market and the firms with lower market shares simply follow the pricing changes prompted by the dominant firm. We see examples of this with the major Building Societies and Petrol retailers where most suppliers follow the pricing strategies of leading firms.

SUMMARY OF KEY CHARACTERISTICS

Characteristic	Perfect Competition	Monopolistic Competition	Oligopoly	Monopoly
Number of firms	Many	Many	Few	One
Type of product	Homogeneous	Differentiated	Differentiated	Limited due to lack of competition
Barriers to entry	None	None	High	High
Abnormal short run profit	✓	✓	✓	✓
Abnormal long run profit	✗	✗	✓	✓
Pricing	Price taker	Price maker	Price maker	Price maker
Profit maximiser	✓	✓	Not always	Usually, but not always
Non price competition	✗	✓	✓	✓
Economic efficiency	High	Relatively high	Low	Low

A DETAILED EXAMINATION OF PERFECT COMPETITION AND MONOPOLY

THE SHORT-RUN EQUILIBRIUM UNDER PERFECT COMPETITION

The very strong assumptions required to create a perfectly competitive market mean that firms operate in a unique environment. The fact that there is perfect knowledge and homogeneous products mean that all firms are **price takers**. They face a **perfectly elastic demand** curve. If any firm raises its prices demand will fall to zero as consumers, with perfect knowledge, switch to other producers. Diagram 6.2, shows the short run equilibrium for perfect competition.

Diagram 6.2

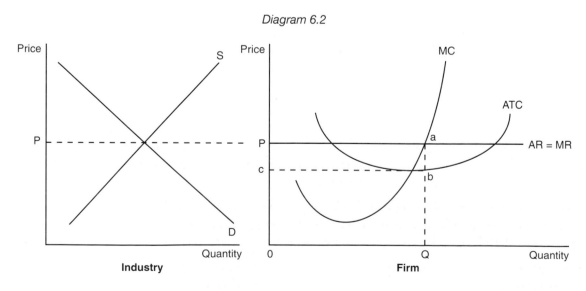

In the **short run,** the twin forces of market demand and market supply determine the equilibrium market price in the industry. In Diagram 6.2 a price P is established and this price is taken by each of the firms. The average revenue curve (AR) is their individual demand curve. Since the market price is constant for each unit sold, the AR curve also becomes the marginal revenue curve (MR).

For the firm shown in the diagram the profit maximising output is at Q where MC = MR. This output generates a **total revenue** (P x Q) equal to OPaQ. The **total cost** of producing this output can be calculated by multiplying the average cost of a unit of output (bQ) and the output produced. Total costs will therefore be equal to OcbQ. Since the total revenue exceeds total cost the firm is making **abnormal profits** (see Chapter 5). This is not necessarily the case for all firms. It depends on the position of their short run cost curves. Some firms may be experiencing **sub-normal profits** if average costs exceed the ruling market price. For these firms, total costs will be greater than total revenue.

THE ADJUSTMENT TO THE LONG-RUN EQUILIBRIUM FOR THE INDUSTRY

Diagram 6.3

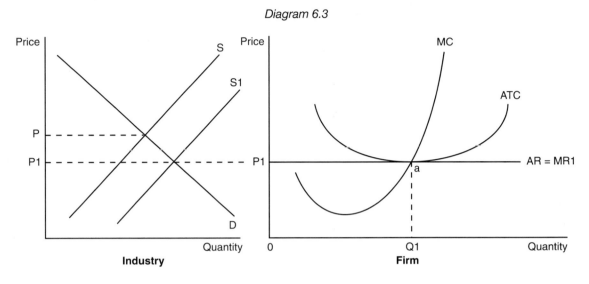

If most firms are making **abnormal profits** in the short run this will encourage the **entry of new firms** into the industry. This will cause an outward shift in **the market supply curve** from S to S1, and force down the market price to P1. This is illustrated in Diagram 6.3. The new profit-maximising output is now Q1. The increase in market supply has reduced the ruling market price until the **price = long run average cost**. At this point each firm is making **normal profits** only. This is because total revenue and total costs are the same and both equal to OP1aQ. There is no further incentive for movement of firms in and out of the industry and **a long run equilibrium** has been established.

PERFECT COMPETITION AND ECONOMIC EFFICIENCY

Perfect competition is used as a yardstick to compare with other market structures because it displays high levels of economic efficiency. In both the short and long run, price is equal to marginal cost (P = MC) and **allocative efficiency** is achieved. **Productive efficiency** occurs when price is equal to average cost at its minimum point. This is not achieved in the short run, but is attained in the long run. The long run of perfect competition, therefore, exhibits **optimal levels of economic efficiency**.

SUMMARY TABLE

	Short run	Long run
Allocative efficiency (P = MC)	✓	✓
Productive efficiency (P = ATC at min)	✗	✓

MONOPOLY

A pure monopolist is the sole supplier in an industry and, as a result, the monopolist can take the market demand curve as its own demand curve. A monopolist therefore faces a downward sloping AR curve with a

MR curve with twice the gradient of AR. (refer back to Chapter 5). The firm is a price maker and has some power over the setting of **price or output**. It cannot, however, charge a price that the consumers in the market will not bear. Assuming that the firm aims to maximise profits (where MR = MC) we establish a short run equilibrium as shown in Diagram 6.4.

Diagram 6.4

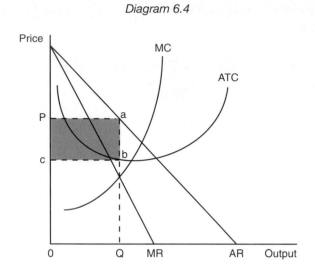

The profit-maximising level of output is at Q and the firm will charge price P. This will generate total revenue equal to OPaQ, but the cost of producing this output will be OcbQ. As total revenue exceeds total costs the firm will generate abnormal profits equal to Pabc. These profits can be earned in both the short and long run because of **barriers to entry**. No new competition will be able to enter the market and dilute the profit.

Monopoly and economic efficiency

Monopolists earn abnormal profits at the expense of economic efficiency. Price is higher than both marginal and average costs and, as a result, **neither allocative nor productive efficiency is achieved**.

The monopolist is extracting a price from consumers that is above the cost of resources used in making the product. The needs and wants of consumers are not being satisfied as the product is being under-consumed. The high average cost of production means that the firm is not making optimum use of scarce resources.

A COMPARISON BETWEEN PURE MONOPOLY AND PERFECT COMPETITION

Diagram 6.5

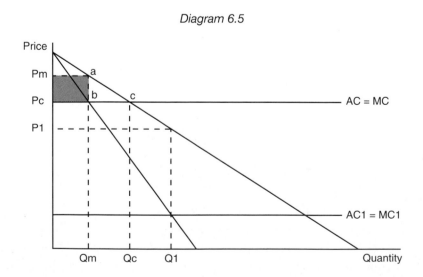

The conventional view when comparing price and output under both pure monopoly and perfect competition is that **a monopolist will produce a lower output at a higher price** than a competitive industry.

42

Diagram 6.5 assumes that there are constant costs for both industries. This means that the average cost curve and marginal cost curve is effectively the industry's supply curve. The perfectly competitive industry will produce in the long run where **market demand (AR) = market supply (AC = MC)**. The equilibrium output and price is at Qc and Pc. At this point, P = MC and the industry is allocatively efficient.

If the industry is taken over by a **monopolist** (who takes the demand curve AR) the **profit-maximising point** (MC = MR) is at price Pm and output Qm. The monopolist will charge a **higher price and reduce both output and the overall level of economic welfare**. The rise in price to Pm **reduces consumer surplus** by the area PcPmac. Some of this reduction in consumer welfare is transferred to the producer in the form of higher profits, (this is the shaded area) but some of the loss is not reassigned to any other economic agent. This is known as the **deadweight welfare loss** and is equal to area abc. The monopolist is also **allocatively inefficient** as it is pricing above marginal cost.

This approach however discounts the possibility that the monopolist might be better able to exploit **economies of scale**. If the monopolist moves onto AC1 and MC1 when average costs fall, a new equilibrium will be established. The profit maximising equilibrium is now at output Q1 and price P1. This is a higher output and a lower price than under perfect competition. In this scenario, consumers actually benefit from a monopoly. Supporters of monopolies would also argue consumers can benefit in other ways. As firms are able to earn **abnormal profits** in the long run there may be a faster rate of technological development that will **reduce costs** and produce **better quality products for consumers**. This is because the monopolist will invest profits into research and development to promote **dynamic efficiency**.

An opposing argument is that the **lack of competition** gives a monopolist no incentive to invest in new ideas or consider consumer welfare. It can also be argued that even if a monopolist were to benefit from economies of scale they will have little incentive to control costs and **'X' inefficiencies** will mean that there will be no real cost savings. Critics also highlight the fact that even if economies of scale manage to lower prices for consumers, the price charged is still above marginal costs and **allocative inefficiency exists**.

PRICE DISCRIMINATION UNDER MONOPOLY

A monopolist may be able to engage in a policy of **price discrimination.** This occurs when a firm charges different prices to different groups of consumers for an identical good or service. It is important to stress that charging different prices for similar goods is not price discrimination. For example, price discrimination does not occur when a rail company charges a higher price for a first class seat. This is because the price premium over a second class seat can be explained by differences in the cost of providing the service.

Conditions required for price discrimination to work

▶ There must be a different **price elasticity of demand** for the product from each group of consumers. The firm will then charge a higher price to the group with a more inelastic demand and charge a lower price to the group with a more elastic demand. By adopting such a strategy, the firm will increase its total revenue and profits.

▶ The firm must be able to prevent **market seepage**. This is where consumers who purchase a good or service at a lower price resell it to those consumers who would have paid the higher price.

▶ The **costs of selling** to different sub-groups (or market segments) must not be prohibitive.

▶ The **monopolist must have control over the sale of the product with price setting power.** This is true by definition with monopoly. Price discrimination could not happen in a perfectly competitive market!

PERFECT PRICE DISCRIMINATION

With perfect (or first degree) price discrimination the firm separates the whole market into individual consumers and charges them the maximum price they are **willing to pay**. This is indicated by the demand curve. If successful, the firm can extract all of the consumer surplus lying beneath the demand curve and turn it into extra revenue. This is impossible to achieve unless the firm knows every consumer's preferences and, as a result, is unlikely to occur in the real world.

SECOND DEGREE PRICE DISCRIMINATION – EXCESS CAPACITY PRICING

This type of price discrimination is when a firm sells off any excess capacity that it has at a price that is lower than the normal published price. Good examples of this phenomenon can be found in the hotel and airline industries where spare rooms and seats are sold on a last minute standby basis.

In these types of industries, the **fixed costs** of production (the costs that do not vary with output) are very high. For example, the high costs of building a hotel or leasing a plane are clearly fixed. At the same time the marginal costs in these industries are relatively small and constant. Marginal costs are the costs of providing an additional unit of output, for example an extra hotel room or airline seat.

In these industries, the product can be provided at a constant marginal cost until a rigid **physical capacity limit** is reached. This means the marginal cost (MC) curve will be horizontal up to full capacity. At this point, the marginal cost curve will become vertical, as it is impossible to provide any additional output. This is illustrated in Diagram 6.6.

Diagram 6.6

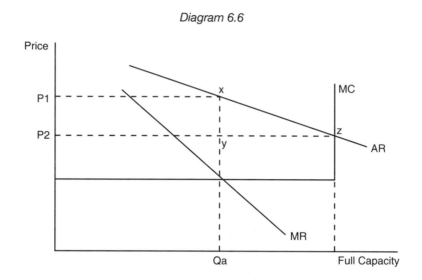

The firm initially produces where **MC = MR** (profit maximisation) charging price P1 and producing at quantity Qa. In this circumstance the firm has a large amount of **spare capacity** equal to the difference between Qa and full capacity. The firm can then sell this excess capacity on a last minute standby basis at the lower price P2. This benefits consumers who are able to purchase the service at the last minute as they pay a lower price. This will **increase total consumer surplus** by the area xyz.

The **firm will also benefit** as there is no point leaving hotel rooms or airline seats empty. A hotel must remain open, and a plane must fly, even if there are only a few paying customers. Providing the revenue received from the extra units sold is greater than the marginal cost of those units, the firm will be **contributing towards its fixed costs** or even **adding to its profit**.

Second degree price discrimination can be seen in many different markets where excess capacity needs to be eliminated. The traditional end of season sale is perhaps the simplest example. Other good examples include cheaper car rental at weekends, reduced cinema and theatre tickets in the afternoon and last minute reductions in the holiday market.

THIRD DEGREE PRICE DISCRIMINATION

This is the most frequently found form of discrimination and involves charging different prices for the same product in different segments of the market. The market is usually separated in two ways: by time or by geography.

▶ Telephone and electricity companies separate markets by time: There are three rates for telephone calls: a daytime peak rate, an off-peak evening rate and a cheaper weekend rate. Electricity suppliers also offer cheaper off-peak electricity during the night.

▶ Markets can also be separated by geography. For example, exporters may charge a higher price in overseas markets if demand is more inelastic than it is in home markets.

Suppose that a firm has separated a market by time into a peak market with inelastic demand, and an off-peak market with elastic demand. The demand and marginal revenue curves for the peak market and off-peak markets are labelled a and b respectively. This is illustrated in Diagram 6.7.

Diagram 6.7

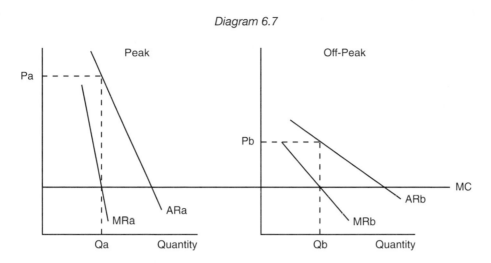

Assuming a constant marginal cost for supplying to each group of consumers, the firm aims to charge a profit maximising price to each group. In the peak market the firm will produce where MRa = MC and charge price Pa, and in the off-peak market the firm will produce where MRb = MC and charge price Pb. Consumers with an inelastic demand for the product will pay a higher price (Pa) than those with an elastic demand who will be charged Pb.

DOES PRICE DISCRIMINATION WORK IN THE INTERESTS OF CONSUMERS?

▶ **Consumer surplus** is reduced in most cases – representing a loss of consumer welfare.

▶ However some consumers who can buy the product at a lower price may benefit. Previously they may have been excluded from consuming the good.

▶ In most cases price is greater than marginal cost and therefore firms are **not achieving allocative efficiency.**

▶ Price discrimination is clearly in the interests of firms who achieve **higher profits**.

▶ The profits made in one market may allow firms to **cross-subsidise** loss-making activities/services that have important **social benefits**. For example, profits made on commuter services may allow railway companies to support loss making rural or night time services. Without the ability to price-discriminate these services may have to be withdrawn.

THE CONCEPT OF CONTESTABLE MARKETS

There are some markets where economists believe that even if there is a monopoly the benefits of competition can still be realised. These are known as **contestable markets**. For a contestable market to exist there must be low **barriers to entry and exit**. Indeed, if entry is easy, then the existence of a very few firms, or even only one firm, may not result in economic inefficiency. **A perfectly contestable market** is one in which entry and exit are absolutely costless. In such a market, competitive pressures supplied by the perpetual threat of entry, as well as by the presence of actual current rivals, can prevent monopoly behaviour (higher prices and restricted output).

If entry is not easy, and there are significant **barriers to entry**, the threat of competition is less. Barriers to entry exist when there are **sunk costs**, expenses that cannot be recovered once a firm has entered the industry. Examples for the airline industry include the set up and advertising costs of entering the industry. These cannot be recovered if a firm's entry into a market is unsuccessful. Other fixed costs, traditionally seen as sunk costs, may be recoverable if an airline leases planes and rents hangar space. Where sunk costs are high, new firms will not consider entering a market and the industry will probably operate as the theory of monopoly suggests.

Industries and Markets that have become more contestable in recent years include:

- Electricity and Gas Supply
- Home Banking and Financial Services
- Internet Service Providers
- Low cost domestic airlines
- Online Communications (including video conferencing; virtual reality games; publishing; home shopping; travel services; information services; databases)
- Road Haulage Companies

Chapter 7
MARKET FAILURE

The market mechanism will not always lead to an optimum allocation of resources, and this is known as **market failure**. There are many different reasons why markets might fail, but here we will explore the four main causes:

- Monopoly power
- Negative externalities
- Positive externalities and merit goods
- Public goods

MONOPOLY POWER

In Chapter 6, the concentration of market power was seen to result in **higher prices** and **lower output**. Monopolists can earn abnormal profits at **the expense of economic efficiency**. Price is greater than both marginal and average costs and, as a result, neither allocative nor productive efficiency is achieved.

If monopolies exploit consumers the government can intervene to **protect consumers' interests**. This intervention can take several different forms:

Competition Commission – the commission is empowered to investigate mergers and takeovers. They will block them if they think the mergers and takeovers will result in excessive monopoly power that will be against the interests of consumers. The proposed merger of Abbey National and Lloyds TSB was blocked on these grounds in 2001.

The Office of Fair Trading (OFT) – is responsible for enforcing the United Kingdom's competition policy and protecting the welfare of consumers. Its main roles are:

▶ To **investigate** the activities of industry and commerce and **remedy anti-competitive practices** and **abuses of market power**. One of the most common anti-competitive practices is predatory pricing, where a dominant firm cuts its prices until it forces competing businesses out of the market. The firm will then raise its prices to exploit its monopoly position.

▶ To **correct trading practices that are against the consumers' interests**. For example, in 2001 the OFT ordered the newly privatised energy companies to stop mis-selling and pressurising people into entering contracts for their products.

▶ To **regulate the provision of consumer credit**.

Utility Regulators – the government has appointed regulators to oversee the activities of companies privatised over the last two decades. These former state owned utilities are regulated to ensure that they do not exploit their monopoly position. Examples of regulation include:

▶ The introduction of **price capping.**

▶ The **introduction of competition into markets** – although this has not been possible in the water market. Competition was introduced into the telecommunications market in 1984; in gas from 1996-98 and in electricity in 1998.

▶ Monitoring the **quality of service provision** and improving standards for consumers.

NEGATIVE EXTERNALITIES

Externalities are common in virtually all economic activities. They are defined as **third party** (or spill over) **effects** arising from the **production** and/or **consumption** of goods and services for which no appropriate compensation is paid.

Externalities can cause **market failure** if the **price mechanism** does not take into account the full **social costs** and **social benefits** of production and consumption. The study of externalities by economists has become extensive in recent years, not least because of concerns about the link between the economy and the environment.

THE DIFFERENCE BETWEEN PRIVATE AND SOCIAL COSTS

Externalities create a divergence between the **private** and **social costs** of production.

> **SOCIAL COST = PRIVATE COST + EXTERNALITY**

▶ **Private costs** are the costs to a firm of producing a good or service and to an individual of consuming a product.

▶ **External costs** are the spill over effects on third parties.

▶ **Social costs** are obtained by adding the private and external costs together. They reflect the total cost to society of an economic decision.

External costs and social costs are not the same concepts, although all too frequently they are confused.

EXAMPLE: PRIVATE AND EXTERNAL COSTS AND BENEFITS OF CAR OWNERSHIP

PRIVATE COSTS
- Purchase of vehicle
- Road taxes
- Insurance
- Running costs: maintenance, fuel and depreciation

PRIVATE BENEFITS
- Satisfaction of running a privately owned car
- Increased mobility and flexibility of lifestyle
- Convenience

EXTERNAL COSTS OF CAR OWNERSHIP
- Traffic congestion reduces average speeds and lengthens journey times.
- Slower journeys increase transportation costs for goods and services and add to the overall cost of living in the economy. This makes domestic firms less competitive.
- High accident rates in areas with congested traffic impose extra costs on the National Health Service. Another major problem is air pollution, which causes asthma and heart attacks.

EXTERNAL BENEFITS OF CAR OWNERSHIP
- Output of the motor car industry generates employment and income in the economy.
- The motor car industry creates hundreds of thousands of jobs in related **complementary industries:**
  - Vehicle insurance
  - Repair and Maintenance
  - Petrol Retailing
  - Design industries
- High levels of tax on petrol bring in very large amounts of tax revenue for the Treasury each year.

MARKET FAILURE WITH NEGATIVE EXTERNALITIES FROM PRODUCTION

When negative production externalities exist, **social marginal cost > private marginal cost.**

Common external costs arising from production include:
- Noise
- Atmospheric and water pollution
- Visual intrusion
- Congestion

Consider the following example of a firm producing negative externalities. A chemical factory discharges its waste products into a local river. This **kills off the fish stock** and causes **illness** amongst water sports' enthusiasts who use the river for recreational purposes.

A profit maximising firm will **ignore these external costs** when determining its price and output strategy and focus purely on the private costs and benefits. Clearly, there is a divergence between the private and social costs of production.

When negative externalities exist, the social marginal cost (SMC) will be greater than the private marginal cost (PMC). This is because the cost to society of each additional unit of output is greater than that experienced by the chemical producer. This is illustrated in Diagram 7.1.

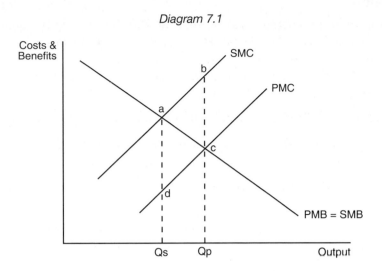

Diagram 7.1

A market failure problem is likely to exist because the cost to society in terms of the deterioration of the environment is unpriced by the price mechanism. This leads to the **privately optimal level of output being greater than the socially optimal** level of production.

The **private optimum** occurs where the **private marginal benefit** (the benefit to the firm of producing the last unit) **equals the private marginal cost**, giving an output of **Qp**. At this level of output, the distance bc represents the size of the external costs that are ignored by the producer.

If we assume that there are no positive externalities, then private marginal benefit will be equal to social marginal benefit. As a result, in terms of social efficiency, we have an **excess supply of output**. The socially optimal level of output in this industry occurs where **SMB = SMC**. At this point, the effects of chemical production on the environment are considered. If we sum up the excess of SMC over SMB between Qs and Qp, we arrive at a figure which gives an indication of the **deadweight welfare loss to society** of the current private level of output. This is the triangle abc. Society as a whole could be made better off by reducing the current level of output from Qp to Qs.

CORRECTING FOR NEGATIVE EXTERNALITIES

When externalities are present the individual pursuit of **self interest** rarely results in **maximum social welfare**. When it does not, we have an outcome that is, by definition, inefficient. This, in turn, means that it is possible to rearrange things in a way that makes some people, at least, better off without harming others in the process. There is an economic rationale for some form of **government intervention** in markets where externalities are prevalent.

How can we take into account the third party effects that necessarily arise? The key is to **internalise the externalities** that exist – to force the firms and consumers that create the externalities to **take them into account** when making their decisions. Policy options open to governments include:

TAXATION

One of the most common policies used to tackle the problem of pollution is the so-called **green or environmental tax**. A tax is placed on a product that damages the environment, or on a complementary product, in an attempt to reduce its production or consumption. Examples of green taxes include: petrol tax, vehicle excise duty, landfill tax, and the new carbon tax.

The idea of using taxes to make the '**polluter pay**' towards the damage that is caused to the environment was developed by the economist A.C. Pigou. The aim of an environmental tax is **to increase the firm's private marginal cost** (PMC) until it equates with the social marginal cost curve (SMC). This will result in a socially efficient level of output. In Diagram 7.1, this would mean setting a tax equal to the distance ad, which is equal to the level of environmental damage caused at the optimum level of output.

Problems with taxation

1. There are many **problems in setting a tax** so that the PMC will exactly equate with the SMC. The government cannot accurately calculate the private benefits and cost of firms let alone put a monetary value on externalities. Without **accurate information** in all these areas, setting the tax at the correct level is virtually impossible. In reality, therefore, all that governments and regulatory agencies can hope to achieve is a movement towards the optimum level of output.

2. Taxes **reduce output and raise prices**, and this will have an adverse effect on consumer welfare.

3. Producers may be able to pass on the tax to the consumers if the demand for the good is inelastic and, as a result, the tax may only have a **marginal effect in reducing output**.

4. Taxes on some de-merit goods may have a **regressive** effect (see Chapter 11) and will widen the distribution of income.

5. If taxes are raised in one country producers may shift production to countries with lower taxes. This will not reduce global pollution, and may create problems such as **unemployment and a lack of competitiveness.**

REGULATION

Taxes are certainly not the only policies that can be implemented to reduce pollution. The government can intervene and directly **regulate** the level of output and pollution in a market. In theory, the government could set a **quota** (a physical limit on output) so that output is set at the **social optimum**.

The use of minimum environmental standards is widespread in many industries. This form of regulation requires regulatory bodies to inspect and fine firms that do not meet the **standards set for water and air quality**. The 1989 Environmental Protection Act set standards on emissions for firms that carried out chemical processes, waste incineration and oil refining.

Problems with regulation

▶ Like taxes, it is very hard to set a quota without accurate estimates for private benefits, costs and environmental damage. This means that, realistically, all regulation can hope to achieve is a reduction in environmental damage and a movement towards the optimum level of output.

▶ Regulation can be **costly to enforce** and it may be impossible to monitor all firms accurately.

▶ Some firms may not cut their emissions of pollutants if the fine they receive is less than the benefit they derive from polluting.

▶ If **emissions are banned** this will lead to output being reduced to zero. Output will be reduced to below the socially optimal level of output. **The optimal level of pollution is unlikely to be zero.**

MARKETABLE PERMITS

One of the most recent developments in the field of environmental control is the use of marketable permits to curtail pollution.

A **marketable permit gives a firm the right to emit a given quantity of waste** into the environment. Ideally, the number of permits that are issued corresponds with the level of pollution that is admissible at the optimum level of output, i.e. where the SMB = SMC. Once this has been determined, the permits are issued and firms that pollute the environment can begin to **buy and sell** them amongst themselves.

While the total level of pollution is not affected by these transactions, the cost of pollution control to society is reduced. All firms are given a clear incentive to develop and install the latest pollution control equipment.

▶ Those firms who find it easy to reduce the level of their emissions will do so and sell some of their permits for cash on the open market.

▶ Other firms who find pollution abatement measures relatively expensive compared to the price of permits can buy these from other firms.

Consequently the use of marketable permits minimises the cost of pollution control.

The permit system needs **regulation** and can suffer many of the problems discussed above. Permit schemes are also very hard to operate when many countries are involved.

POSITIVE EXTERNALITIES

Positive externalities are often given less attention than negative externalities but they are very important. When positive externalities exist, **social marginal benefit > private marginal benefit.**

Merit goods exhibit the same features as positive externalities, but they are subtly different. Merit goods are under consumed because of **information failure**. Those consuming services (such as education and healthcare), do not fully appreciate how much benefit they are deriving from the consumption of these services. A private individual will find it difficult to predict the monetary benefits of a good education and, as a result, because of a lack of information, may choose to curtail their schooling.

Positive externalities and merit goods have important **external benefits**. Examples that can be used include:

▶ **Industrial training by firms**: This can reduce the costs faced by other firms and has important effects on labour productivity.

▶ **Education**: A well educated labour force can increase efficiency and produce other important external benefits, such as lower unemployment and greater international competitiveness. Increasingly, policy makers are coming to realise the increased returns that might be exploited from investing in **human capital** at all ages.

▶ **Health provision:** Improved health provision and health care reduces absenteeism and creates a better quality of life and higher living standards.

▶ **Arts and sporting participation:** Visiting museums and theatres can increase **knowledge.** The external benefits of increased knowledge are hard to quantify, but are probably very important. Sporting participation will lead to a healthier nation and improve team working skills.

Where substantial positive externalities exist, the good or service may be **under consumed or under provided** since the free market may fail to take into account the external benefits. This is because the **marginal social benefits** of consuming the good > **private marginal benefits**.

An example of positive externalities arising from the consumption of education is shown in Diagram 7.2. In the example, a consumer benefits from higher education that increases productivity causing SMB to rise.

Diagram 7.2

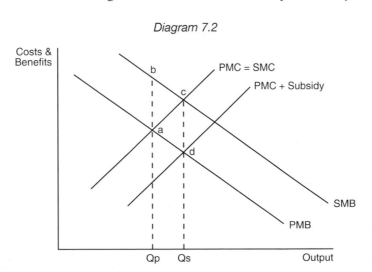

A market failure problem is likely to exist because the benefit to society in terms of higher productivity and a higher GDP is unpriced by the price mechanism. This leads to the **privately optimal level of output being less than the socially optimal** level of production.

The consumer simply does not take into account the external benefits of higher education. The private optimum occurs where the private marginal benefit (the benefit to the individual of consuming the last unit) equals private marginal cost, giving an output of **Qp**. At this level of output, the distance ab represents the size of the external benefit.

If we assume that there are no negative externalities, then PMC will equal the SMC. In terms of social efficiency, education is under consumed. The socially optimal level of output is where **SMB = SMC**. If we sum up the excess of SMB over PMB between Qs and Qp, we arrive at a figure which gives an indication of the **deadweight welfare loss** to society. This is the triangle abc. Society as a whole could be made better off by increasing the current level of output from Qp to Qs.

CORRECTING FOR POSITIVE EXTERNALITIES

Subsidies

Activities that lead to positive externality effects can be **subsidised.** The aim of a subsidy is **to reduce the private marginal cost** (PMC) until it is equal to point d in Diagram 7.2. A subsidy equal to cd would ensure that the socially optimal level of output is achieved. Examples of subsidies and grants include: those given as part of the New Deal for the training of unemployed workers, and grants to museums and sports facilities.

As with taxes it is very hard to set the subsidy. As governments **do not have precise information** on the size of the costs, benefits and external effects associated with positive externalities, all that can be really hoped for is an increase in consumption. The size of the effect of a subsidy will depend on **the price elasticity of demand**. If demand is inelastic, a subsidy will only lead to a small rise in consumption.

Regulation

The best way to ensure the consumption of positive externalities is to provide them free of charge. Education is provided by the state for individuals up to the age of eighteen, as are most healthcare services. This means that everybody, regardless of his or her income, has access to these services. An economist might argue that such a policy is **not economically efficient**. This is because it might encourage consumption to be higher than the socially optimal level of output.

Information

The government may advertise the benefits of merit goods to encourage consumers to increase consumption. By reducing the information failure, consumers may acknowledge that the good or service has greater benefits than they realised and increase consumption. A good example is the advertising of health screening.

PUBLIC GOODS

Public goods are services which are clearly in demand, but which must be provided collectively for two main reasons:

▶ **Non-excludability** – the goods cannot be confined to those who have paid for it.

▶ **Non-rivalry in consumption** – the consumption by one individual does not reduce the availability of goods to others.

Examples of public goods include flood control systems, street lighting and national defence. A flood control system, such as the Thames Barrier, cannot be confined to those who have paid for the service. Also the consumption of the service by one household will not reduce its availability to others.

If left to the market mechanism, **no public goods would be provided** and, as a result, there would be **market failure**. No consumer would pay for a product that could be consumed for free if another household decided to purchase it.

Quasi-public goods are products that are public in nature, but **do not exhibit fully the features of non-excludability and non-rivalry**. The road network in the UK is currently available to all, but could be made excludable via a system of tolls. There is also non-rivalry in consumption, but only up to an extent. Once the road becomes congested there is rivalry in consumption.

Chapter 8
NATIONAL INCOME CALCULATIONS & EQUILIBRIUM

National Income measures the value of output produced within the economy over a period of time. One of the key economic objectives of government is to increase the level, and rate of growth, of national income. Before we start to analyse why economic growth is so important, it is important to be able to define the key concepts.

GROSS DOMESTIC PRODUCT (GDP)

Under new definitions introduced in the late 1990s, **Gross Domestic Product** is also known as **Gross Value Added**. It is defined as the **value of output produced within the domestic boundaries of the UK** over a given period of time, usually a year. It includes the output of foreign owned firms that are located in the UK, such as Nissan in Sunderland and Toyota in Derby. It does not include output of UK firms that are located abroad. There are three ways of calculating the value of GDP – all of which should sum to the same amount since by identity:

NATIONAL OUTPUT = NATIONAL INCOME = NATIONAL EXPENDITURE

1. THE EXPENDITURE METHOD

This is the sum of the final expenditure on UK produced goods and services measured at current market prices (not adjusted for inflation). The full equation for calculating GDP using this approach is:

GDP = Consumer expenditure (C) + Investment (I) + Government expenditure (G) + (Exports (X) – Imports (M))

The definition of each of the components of GDP will be given later in the Chapter.

2. THE INCOME METHOD

This is the **sum of total incomes** earned from the production of goods and services. By adding together **the rewards to the factors of production** (land, labour, capital and enterprise), we can see how the flow of income in the economy is distributed. The rewards to the factors of production can be loosely summarised in the following table:

Factor	Reward
Land	Rent
Labour	Wages and salaries
Capital	Interest
Enterprise	Profit

Only those incomes generated through the production of a marketed output are included in the calculation of GDP by the income approach. Therefore we exclude from the accounts items such as **transfer payments** (e.g. government benefits for jobseekers allowance and pensions where no output is produced) and **private transfers of money**.

The income method tends to underestimate the true value of output in the economy, as incomes earned through the **black economy** are not recorded.

3. THE OUTPUT MEASURE OF GDP

This measures the value of output produced by each of the productive sectors in the economy (primary, secondary and tertiary) using the concept of **value added.**

Value added is the increase in the value of a product at each successive stage of the production process. For example, if the raw materials and components used to make a car cost £6,000 and the final selling price of the car is £10,000, then the value added from the production process is £4,000. We use this approach to avoid the problems of **double-counting** the value of intermediate inputs. GDP will, therefore, be equal to the sum of each individual producer's value added.

THE DIFFERENCE BETWEEN GDP AND GNI

Under the new definitions, **Gross National Product** (GNP) is now known as **Gross National Income** (GNI). It measures the **value of income from UK owned factors of production** over a given period of time, usually a year. GNI is concerned with incomes generated by all UK owned factors of production whether they are located in the UK or overseas. It excludes the output of foreign owned firms that are located in the UK, but includes the output of UK firms located abroad.

> GNI = GDP + Net property income from abroad (NPIA)

NPIA is the net balance of **interest, profits and dividends (IPD)** coming into the UK from UK assets owned overseas matched against the outflow of profits and other incomes from foreign owned assets located within the UK. For example, if a British-owned company operating in Germany sends some of its profits back to the UK this adds to UK GNI. Similarly, when a Japanese company located in the UK sends profits to Japan this will reduce UK GNI.

GDP at MARKET PRICES and GDP at BASIC PRICES (Factor Cost)

The value of **marketed output** produced within the economy is affected by the imposition of indirect taxes and subsidies by the Government. Taxes **artificially inflate** the prices of goods whilst subsidies **cause the market price to fall below the true basic prices.** Therefore to adjust for this:

> GDP at market prices – Indirect taxes + subsidies = GDP at basic prices (formerly known as factor cost)

THE STANDARD OF LIVING

One of the main uses of national income figures is in measuring the economic wellbeing or standard of living of the population. Living standards are assessed by looking at **real GDP per person** (per capita). Firstly, **money or nominal GDP** (also known as GDP at current market prices) must be converted into **real GDP** (also known as GDP at constant prices).

MONEY GDP and REAL GDP

When we want to measure the **real rate of growth** in the economy we have to adjust for the **effects of inflation**. Real GDP/GNI measures the level and rate of growth of the **volume of output produced within the economy.** If expenditure on goods and services has risen faster than the rate of price inflation, then the volume of output has increased. This means the economy is experiencing **positive economic growth**.

It is vital to look at real GDP or GNI when analysing living standards. This is because figures expressed in money, or nominal terms, can give a very distorted picture. For example, if money GDP grows by 2%, it may appear that output in the economy is increasing. If, however, prices had increased by 4% over the same period of time, then the volume of output would have fallen by 2% and the economy would have contracted. The formula below shows how to convert money GDP to real GDP:

> REAL GDP or GNI = Money GDP or GNI x 100 / Price Index (GDP deflator)

When we convert money GDP to real GDP, or GDP at constant prices, we are adjusting for the effects of inflation by keeping prices at the same level as they were in a selected **base year**. Suppose that, in 2002, a country's money GDP was £500bn and the price index was 100 (base year). If, in 2003, money GDP rises to £530bn and the price index increases by 5% to 105; using the formula above, real GDP in 2003 is £530bn x (100/105) = £504.8bn.

REAL GDP PER CAPITA

To convert real GDP to a **per capita figure**, real GDP must be **divided by the size of the population**. This gives an indication of income per head and is the starting point for assessing living standards. The limitations of using this measure to assess the economic welfare of a population are shown below:

▶ National GDP figures hide significant **regional variations** in output, employment and incomes. Within each region there are also areas of prosperity contrasting with **unemployment blackspots**. For example, London has a per capita income that is 30% above the UK average, but it also has five boroughs with some of the highest unemployment rates in the UK.

▶ GDP figures on their own do not show the **distribution of income and wealth**. Real GDP per capita only gives us an indication of average incomes but, in reality, incomes are unequally distributed amongst the population.

The degree of inequality in an economy can be examined by looking at the **Lorenz Curve**. In Diagram 8.1, the cumulative percentage of income is plotted along the y-axis and the cumulative percentage of the population is plotted along the x-axis. A diagonal 45° line represents complete equality in income distribution because the poorest 10% of the population receive 10% of the income, while the richest 10% also only receive 10% of the income.

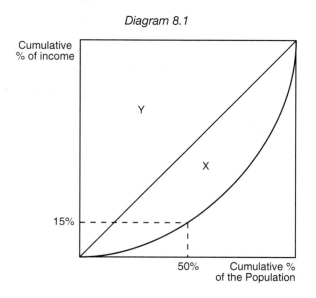

Diagram 8.1

The further the curve bows away from 45°, the greater the level of inequality. In this diagram there is significant inequality as the poorest 50 % of the population only earn 15% of total income. There is a numerical measure of inequality derived from the Lorenz Curve called the **Gini Coefficient**.

This is calculated by dividing area X by area Y in the diagram. Area X lies between the Lorenz Curve and the 45° line while Y is the total area above the 45° line. If the Gini coefficient is **zero** then there is complete **equality** and if it is **one** there is **total inequality** (one person enjoys all the income). It is easy to remember that the greater the Gini Coefficient the more the inequality.

▶ **Externalities** affect the quality of life (see Chapter 7). Rising national output might have been accompanied by an increase in pollution which has a detrimental impact on the welfare of the population.

▶ Output figures tell us little about the **quality of goods and services** produced. A rise in output may not increase living standards if the quality of goods and services has diminished.

▶ Rising national output might have been achieved at the expense of **leisure time** if workers are working longer hours. In the UK the average working week is nearly 44 hours, well above the EU mean. Even though incomes per head may be higher than some EU countries, the opportunity cost of this may be a longer working week, which may reduce the quality of life.

▶ We need to analyse where an increase in GDP comes from before establishing whether or not it will improve living standards. Some economists believe that **the ultimate reason for production is consumption**. If this is the case, a rise in investment will not increase consumption or living standards today. It may, however, boost living standards in the future because higher investment will allow more goods and services to be produced. A rise in exports will increase GDP, but as the output is consumed abroad it could be argued that living standards have not increased. Conversely, a rise in imports reduces GDP, but allows higher consumption and could therefore boost the standard of living.

▶ Faster economic growth might improve living standards today but lead to an **over-exploitation of scarce finite economic resources**, thereby limiting growth prospects, in the future.

▶ GDP figures might **understate** the true living standards because of the existence and growth of the **black economy**. It is estimated that around 15% of output in developed countries is not recorded.

To come to a more general judgement on living standards we can use a range of alternative indicators. These could include:

▶ Ownership of **consumer durables** such as televisions, dishwashers and home computers. The problem with this indicator is that it shows what consumers have chosen to purchase and not necessarily what they can afford to buy.

▶ **Social welfare indicators**. There are a vast number of indicators that could be examined to give a broader assessment of the quality of life. These include the number of patients per doctor, infant mortality rates, the average food intake per person, literacy rates, average educational attainment and crime rates. These statistics should also indicate what proportion of the population is enjoying a **minimum standard of living**. The problem however is that perceptions of what is needed for a basic quality of life vary widely.

▶ **Environmental indicators** such as the amount of pollution created through both production and consumption. High levels of pollution have an adverse effect on economic welfare.

OTHER MEASURES OF LIVING STANDARDS

Since the 1970s, criticism of real GDP per head as an indicator of living standards has been growing. A number of alternative measures have been developed.

▶ The United Nations introduced the **Human Development Index** in 1990. As well as incorporating GDP, the index also uses adult literacy rates, the average number of years schooling and life expectancy to give an indicator of living standards.

▶ **The Index of Sustainable Economic Welfare** adjusts GNI figures by accounting for the decline in natural resources and money spent on correcting environmental damage. By taking these factors into account it is hoped that the index gives a better indication of sustainable living standards in the future.

THE CIRCULAR FLOW OF INCOME

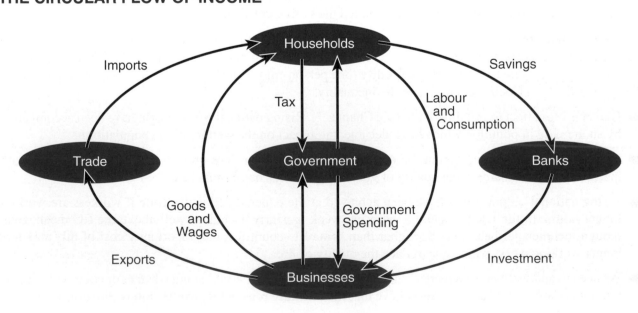

The **circular flow of income and spending** illustrates, in a very simple way, the linkages between the different sectors of the macro economy. The main flow is consumer spending by households on the goods produced by domestic firms. This output generates wages that are used by the household sector to purchase goods and services.

There are three other crucial components to the circular flow:

▶ Households **save** at banks and other financial institutions. This money can then be lent out to firms for **investment** projects.

▶ The government sector is also important through their **taxation and spending** decisions.

▶ There is spending on **imported** goods and services and injections of demand into the economy from the sale of **exports**.

INJECTIONS AND WITHDRAWALS

The circular flow of income highlights the main injections and withdrawals in an economy. These are outlined below:

INJECTIONS	WITHDRAWALS
Exports (X)	Imports (M)
Investment (I)	Savings (S)
Government spending (G)	Taxation (T)

Injections will add money to the circular flow of income while withdrawals will remove money from it. If **injections are greater than withdrawals**, expenditure on goods and services will exceed the planned level of production. Firms will, therefore, expand output and **national income will rise**. Conversely if **withdrawals are greater than injections**, production will exceed the current level of expenditure. Firms will, therefore, reduce their output and **national income will fall**.

When injections equal withdrawals, there will be no tendency for national income to change. This is referred to as **national income equilibrium**. Nowadays students are asked to represent national income equilibrium by using aggregate demand and aggregate supply analysis.

AGGREGATE DEMAND AND AGGREGATE SUPPLY

Equilibrium national income is where the **aggregate demand** (AD) for the economy's goods and services is just equal to the **aggregate supply** (AS) **produced**.

THE AGGREGATE DEMAND CURVE

Aggregate Demand is the **total spending on goods and services** in an economy over a given period of time. It is calculated using the following formula:

AD = Consumer expenditure (C) + Investment (I) + Government expenditure (G) + (Exports (X) – Imports (M))

The components of AD are the same as those used to calculate GDP via the expenditure method, and these are outlined below:

C	**Consumer spending** – is spending on goods and services that are used for the **direct satisfaction** of individual or collective needs. It is also known as **household final consumption expenditure**. This includes personal expenditure on durable and non-durable goods, as well as on services.
I	**Gross Domestic Fixed Capital Formation** – is investment spending on assets that are used repeatedly or continuously over a number of years to produce goods. For example, spending by companies on **capital goods** such as machinery and vehicles. Investment also includes spending on **working capital** such as **stocks** of finished goods and work in progress.

G	**General Government Final Consumption** is current spending on publicly provided goods and services. It also includes spending on public sector employment.
X	**Exports of goods and services** – this is UK produced output that is sold abroad. Exports are an **injection** into the circular flow of income.
M	**Imports of goods and services** – this is foreign produced output that is purchased by UK consumers and firms. Imports are a **withdrawal** from the circular flow of income.

Diagram 8.2 illustrates an **aggregate demand curve**. It is very much like an ordinary demand curve, but the axes on the diagram are different. National output is placed on the x-axis and the price level is represented on the y-axis.

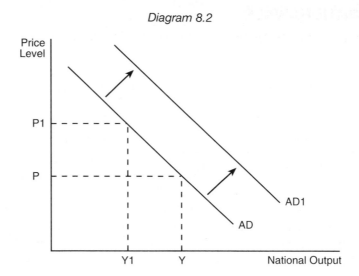

Diagram 8.2

The AD curve is **downward sloping**. A rise in the price level from P to P1 will lead to a fall in the total demand for goods and services from Y to Y1. This is because:

▶ at higher price levels the total demand for goods and services will be lower.

▶ as the price level becomes higher, British goods become **less competitive**. Higher imports and lower exports will reduce AD.

A number of factors will cause the AD curve to shift:

▶ The **aggregate demand curve** will shift to the **right** from AD to AD1 when there is a rise in **consumption, investment, government spending or exports**.

▶ A **rise in imports** will shift the **aggregate demand curve to the left**. This is because imports are a withdrawal from the circular flow of income and will reduce the total demand for UK goods and services.

The factors that influence the components of aggregate demand will be analysed in later Chapters.

THE AGGREGATE SUPPLY CURVE

Aggregate supply (AS) refers to the ability of the economy to provide domestically produced goods at a given price over a given period of time. The **quantity and quality** of the **factors of production** determine the total level of aggregate supply in an economy. The short run AS curve is illustrated in Diagram 8.3.

The AS curve is **upward sloping**. This is because at low price levels many firms will not be able to produce and sell their output profitably. As price levels rise it becomes more profitable for existing firms to expand their output. The total supply of goods and services is further boosted by the fact that new firms now find it profitable to start production. A rise in the price level from P to P1 will lead to an increase in the total supply of goods and services from Y to Y1.

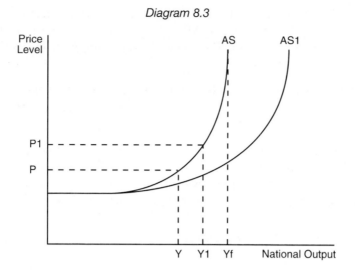

Diagram 8.3

The AS curve is **elastic** (flat) at relatively low levels of output, implying that there are substantial amounts of **spare capacity** in the economy. Output can expand quickly in the short run without a substantial rise in the price level. As the economy moves closer to the **full employment** of the factors of production the AS curve becomes more **inelastic** (steep). Firms start to experience **supply bottlenecks** and there are shortages of raw materials and labour. This means that firms' costs of production start to rise and, in order to maintain their profit margins, they cannot raise production without increasing their prices. Eventually, when all the factors of production are fully employed (at Yf in Diagram 8.3) it is impossible for firms to produce any extra output and the AS curve will become perfectly inelastic. At this point, the economy is operating on its **production possibility frontier** (see Chapter 1). Some economists believe that the **long-run aggregate supply curve** will be **perfectly inelastic** because the quantity and quality of the factors of production determine the maximum potential output of the economy.

The **aggregate supply curve** will shift to the **right** from AS to AS1 when there is an increase in the **quantity**, or an improvement in the **quality**, of the **factors of production**. An increase in the quantity of land, labour, capital or enterprise will result in a rise in the **capacity** of the economy. An improvement in the quality of resources available will mean that a given level of output can be produced at a **lower cost**.

NATIONAL INCOME EQUILIBRIUM

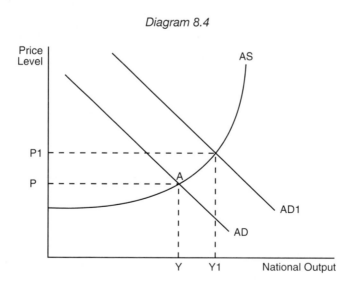

Diagram 8.4

Equilibrium occurs when **aggregate demand equals aggregate supply**. In Diagram 8.4, the AD and AS curves meet at point A. This indicates the equilibrium national output (Y) and price level (P). This is also referred to as the **national income equilibrium**.

If there is a rise in aggregate demand, then the AD curve will shift to the right and a new national income equilibrium will be established at Y1. The rise in AD will cause the price level to rise from P to P1, and the economy is, therefore, experiencing **inflation**. The rise in national output means that there has been **economic growth.**

The increase in inflation may lead to a fall in **international competitiveness**. This may result in a fall in exports and a rise in import penetration. As a result, the current account of the balance of payments (see Chapter 16) may deteriorate.

The concepts of aggregate demand, aggregate supply and national income equilibrium provide a framework that allows us to analyse the economy. In the remaining chapters, AD and AS diagrams will be used to explain how changes in economic policy influence the government's macroeconomic objectives **of high economic growth, low unemployment, low inflation and current account stability.**

THE MULTIPLIER PROCESS AND EFFECT

It is important to remember that a change in aggregate demand will cause a change in national income **greater** than the initial change in expenditure. This is known as the **multiplier effect.**

The multiplier is defined as the ratio of the change in national income to the change in expenditure that brought it about.

Many examples can be used to illustrate the multiplier. Most importantly you must be able to describe in simple terms the **multiplier process**. Consider the effects of an increase in investment by a firm on new machines of £100m. This will raise national income by £100m since the **expenditure of one group is the income of another**. The process will not stop here though. The initial expenditure will **generate incomes** that will be used to finance spending in future time periods. This adds to the effects on total GDP.

At each stage of the process, as income is earned through additional spending, some will leak out of the circular flow of income in the form of **savings** (incomes not spent), **taxation** (taken out by the Government sector) and **imports** (the demand for foreign produced goods and services). Thus the **size of the multiplier effect** is determined by the **rate of leakages or withdrawals** from the economy. To be more specific, the rate at which income is passed on in the form of extra spending within the circular flow is determined by the **marginal propensity to withdrawal** – i.e. the sum of the marginal propensities to save, tax and import. This is the amount of each additional pound earned that is saved; taken in taxes; or spent on imports.

The multiplier process can be outlined with a simple example. It is important to make clear the assumptions of the model. Firstly, we are operating in a simple economy with no government or trade. Secondly the marginal propensity to save for every citizen is 0.5. There is an initial rise in investment spending of £100m. This will immediately increase national income by £100m in time period zero, but we can trace the change in spending and saving in future time periods using the following table.

Time Period	Change in Expenditure (£)	Change in National Income (£)	Saving (£)
0	**100**	100	–
1	50	50	50
2	25	25	25
3	12.5	12.5	12.5
4	6.25	6.25	6.25
		193.75	

In time period 1, 50% of the original rise in national income (£100m) will be saved (£50m), there will be an increase in expenditure of £50m. This will generate an equivalent rise in national income. In time period 2, again 50% of the rise in national income will be saved (£25m), and there will be a further rise in expenditure and national income of £25m. The process goes on. It is illustrated here for four time periods, but in reality it will actually go on until the change in expenditure becomes insignificant. In this simple example, the initial rise in investment was £100m but after only four time periods the total change in national income was £193.75m (£100m + £50m + £25m + £12.5m + £6.25m). It can be seen therefore that a change in aggregate demand has caused a **change in national income greater** than the **initial change in expenditure**.

What is the final change in national income? The answer cannot be calculated unless we obtain a value for the multiplier. The formula for this is provided below along with the answer to this question!

CALCULATING THE VALUE OF THE MULTIPLIER

The multiplier itself is simply a number. The formula for calculating the multiplier **in an open economy with a government sector** is as follows:

Multiplier (m) = 1 / sum of the withdrawals

= 1 / MPS + MPT + MPM

The formula for other more simple economies is as follows:

Simple economy	M = 1/MPS
Closed economy with government (no trade)	M = 1/MPS + MPT

If the marginal propensity to save (MPS) is 0.2, the marginal propensity to tax (MPT) is 0.1 and the marginal propensity to import (MPM) is 0.1, then the sum of the withdrawals in the economy is equal to 0.4. The value of the multiplier will, therefore, be 2.5 (1/0.4).

A **rise in the rate of withdrawals** (or leakages) **reduces the value of the multiplier**. If the MPS = 0.25, the MPT = 0.2 and the MPM = 0.25 then the sum of the withdrawals in the economy = 0.7. Therefore, the value of the multiplier will fall to 1.4 (1/0.7).

CALCULATING THE FINAL CHANGE IN NATIONAL INCOME

The total change in national income arising from an injection into the circular flow can be calculated using the following formula:

Change in expenditure x the value of the multiplier = Change in national income

Going back to our example of a simple economy, there was an increase in investment of £100m. The marginal propensity to save was 0.5 and, therefore, the value of the multiplier is equal to 2. This was calculated by M = 1/MPS; (1/0.5) = 2.

The **final change in national income** will be:

Change in expenditure x the value of the multiplier

£100m x 2 = **£200m**

A rise in the rate of withdrawals (or leakages) reduces the value of the multiplier and the effect of an injection on national income. The size of the multiplier has important consequences for government policy makers and this is discussed further in Chapter 11.

SOME IMPORTANT POINTS ABOUT THE MULTIPLIER

1. It comes into operation for any change in spending. We could be discussing the effects of changes in spending of any or all of C, I, G or X.

2. The multiplier effect also works for **falls in demand**.

3. We have assumed that an increase in aggregate demand does lead to a rise in **real national output**. This is the case when the economy has the **spare capacity** to meet the demand, but there are occasions when any further increase in demand simply creates **inflation**. At this point the economy is close to full capacity and a rise in spending simply fuels **demand-pull inflation**. This is explained in Chapter 13.

4. The estimated value of the multiplier in the UK is around 1.4.

Chapter 9
CONSUMPTION, SAVING AND INVESTMENT

CONSUMER SPENDING

Consumer spending is also known as **household final consumption expenditure**. It includes **personal expenditure** on **durable and non-durable goods** as well as on **services**. Excluded are all business expenditure and expenses, interest payments and spending on dwellings.

Consumers purchase goods and services for the **direct satisfaction** of individual or collective needs, and expenditure on goods and services in the UK accounts for over **60% of GDP**. A change in consumer expenditure will, therefore, have a much greater impact on GDP than a similar variation in another component of aggregate demand.

REAL DISPOSABLE INCOME

In his **absolute income hypothesis**, **J.M. Keynes** highlighted that current **real disposable income** is the most important determinant of **consumer expenditure**.

Real Income is money income adjusted for inflation. For example, if a 5% rise in money income is matched by a 5% rise in inflation then real income has remained constant. This means that the quantity or volume of goods and services that can be bought is unchanged. To make an adjustment to real disposable income, direct taxes and government benefits must be accounted for:

Real Disposable Income (Yd) = gross real income – (deductions from direct taxation + benefits)

The prediction that a rise in real disposable income will lead to a rise in consumer expenditure may not seem to be a remarkable assertion, but Keynes analysed this link in much more detail.

The standard Keynesian consumption function is written as follows:

C = a + cYd where,

C = Consumer expenditure

a = autonomous consumption. This is the level of consumption that would take place even if income was zero. If an individual's income fell to zero some of his existing spending could be sustained by using savings. This is known as **dis-saving**.

c = marginal propensity to consume (mpc). This is the change in consumption divided by the change in income. Simply, it is the percentage of each additional pound earned that will be spent.

OTHER KEY DEFINITIONS

- **Marginal propensity to save** (mps)   = The change in saving divided by the change in income.

- **Average propensity to consume** (apc)   = Total consumption divided by total income.

- **Average propensity to save** (aps)   = Total savings divided by total income (also known as the Saving Ratio).

There are a number of important relationships in Diagram 9.1 that need to be highlighted.

▶ Income (Y) = consumption (C) + saving (S).

▶ The autonomous level of consumption is equal to 'a'. Therefore the savings function must start at '-a', the level of dis-saving when income is zero.

▶ The slope of the consumption function is equal to c, the mpc.

▶ The slope of the savings function is equal to 1-c, the mps.

▶ Note that the **mpc + mps = 1**.

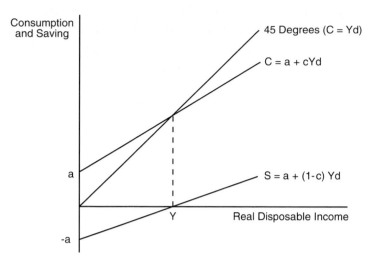

Diagram 9.1

▶ At levels of consumption up to Y, spending is greater than income and the apc is greater than one. This means that dis-saving finances some of the consumption.

▶ At income level Y, spending is equal to income and the apc is equal to one. The apc + aps must equal 1, and, therefore when the apc is equal to one the aps is equal to zero.

▶ At income levels above Y, spending is less than income and the apc is less than one. This implies that savings and the aps are positive.

▶ From the information above, if we are given the consumption function C = 1000 + 0.6Yd, the savings function is very easy to calculate. It must be S = -1000 + 0.4Yd.

SHIFTS IN THE CONSUMPTION AND SAVINGS FUNCTIONS

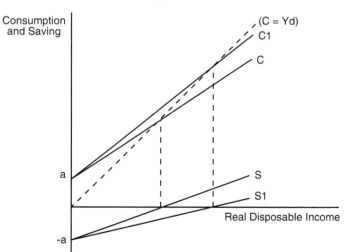

Diagram 9.2

If there is a **fall in interest rates** then consumers may decide to save a smaller part of each additional pound that they earn. As a result, the **mps will fall** and the **mpc will rise**. This is because a fall in the mps must mean that consumers are spending more of each additional pound that they earn. This will cause the gradient of consumption and savings function to change and is illustrated in Diagram 9.2. The consumption function will tilt from C to C1 and become steeper while the savings function will tilt from S to S1 and become flatter.

A change in **autonomous spending** or **saving** would cause the consumption function to shift with the gradient remaining unchanged. This might be caused by an increase in consumer wealth. A rise in house prices should lead to an upward shift in the consumption function. This means that consumers spend more at each level of disposable income. A collapse in share prices will diminish wealth and have the opposite effect.

One clear criticism of the Keynesian model is that, in reality, consumption and saving are not stable functions of real disposable income. The **mpc** tends to be greater at lower levels of disposable income because individuals cannot afford to save a great deal of each additional pound they earn. As disposable incomes increase, individuals can afford to save more of each additional pound and the mpc diminishes. Thus, the **mpc falls with income while the mps increases**. This has important implications. For example, a tax cut to low-income earners will have a greater impact on consumption than a tax cut to high-income earners. This is because low-income earners have a higher mpc.

OTHER FACTORS AFFECTING CONSUMPTION

1. PERMANENT INCOME

According to Milton Friedman, the key determinant of consumption is an individual's **real wealth**, not his current real disposable income. **Permanent income** is determined by a consumer's **assets**; both **physical** (shares, bonds, property) and **human** (education and experience). These assets determine how much a consumer can earn over a lifetime.

Friedman suggests that consumers try to smooth out consumer spending based on their estimates of permanent income. Only if there has been a change in **permanent income** will there be a change in consumption. One key conclusion of this model is that **transitory changes in income do not affect spending behaviour.**

Suppose a government cuts taxes prior to a general election. If consumers perceive this to be only a temporary reduction in their tax burden, purely to boost the government's popularity, then consumption will remain unchanged. If the tax cut is seen to be permanent it will result in an increase in spending.

2. INTEREST RATES

Most students can identify that a **rise in interest rates** will **reduce consumer expenditure**, but few can accurately explain the **transmission mechanisms**. If the Bank of England announces a rise in interest rate there is likely to be:

▶ a **rise in saving**. This is because the **opportunity cost of spending has increased**. If consumers carry on spending they will forego more interest. As a result, saving will probably increase as individuals postpone current consumption in favour of spending in future time periods.

▶ a **fall in demand** for **consumer durables purchased on credit**. This is because **loan repayments**, on items such as TVs, fridges, cars and holidays, **will increase**.

▶ a fall in **'effective disposable incomes'**. A rise in interest rates will increase **mortgage and other loan repayments.** Effectively, this means that consumers are left with less money in their pockets at the end of each month and consumer expenditure will fall.

All these factors should combine to **reduce the demand for assets** such as housing and shares. If the value of assets falls, consumers' wealth will diminish and, as a result, they may cut back on their spending.

3. UNEMPLOYMENT

A rise in the level of unemployment, or the increased threat of being made jobless, may encourage workers to hold higher **precautionary savings**, which will reduce current consumption. Conversely, a fall in unemployment boosts **consumer confidence** and increases spending.

These effects are also reinforced by the fact that changes in **unemployment** influence the **wages and salaries** earned by those in employment. When the demand for labour increases and unemployment falls, the growth of wages and earnings accelerates. This will boost the spending power of people in work and increase consumer expenditure. Rising unemployment in a recession causes a slowdown in income growth and encourages consumers to rein in their spending plans.

4. TAX BURDEN

In theory, a **rise in direct taxes**, such as income tax and national insurance contributions, will reduce **real disposable income** and the level of consumption. A **rise in indirect taxes**, such as VAT, will directly **increase the prices** of goods and services. Consumers are, therefore, likely to cut back expenditure on those products that are affected by the tax, which reduces consumer expenditure.

A tax change may not always have the effect that an economist expects. A **direct tax cut** may not increase consumer expenditure if it is all saved. This may occur if a consumer is uncertain about the future or believes that a tax cut is transitory. Remember, if a tax cut is perceived to be temporary then it will not increase **permanent income** or consumption.

5. POPULATION

The **age structure** of the population has an impact on household consumption. Many economists believe that consumer spending in future years may be limited by the rising number of 30-50 year olds and pensioners in the population. This can be explained by the **life cycle hypothesis**.

This hypothesis is based on the idea that the level of spending relative to income depends on where the consumer is in their **life cycle**. It suggests that consumers attempt to even out consumption over their lifetime and, as a result, will borrow and save at different ages.

► In the 18-30 age range, consumers will spend more than current income. They undertake a large number of credit financed purchases; especially relating to housing.

► In middle age, consumers spend less than current income. They repay their mortgage and other loans and increase **savings** for retirement. This traditional view is becoming less typical in modern society as inheritance and changing family structures, in particular divorce, increasingly influence spending behaviour. Both these factors may stimulate consumption in middle age.

► When consumers reach pensionable age they spend more than their current income. This is because their incomes fall quite sharply and they use up savings made in earlier years.

With fewer people in the 18-30 age group and a growing cohort of pensioners it is possible that the ageing population may slow down aggregate consumption levels in years to come.

6. WEALTH EFFECTS

The **wealth effects** of rising real asset values on consumer expenditure are difficult to quantify, but nevertheless important. When the value of **housing** and other assets (**shares** and **bonds**) is rising faster than income, individuals see a rise in their **net worth** (the difference between the value of their assets and liabilities). This increases consumer confidence and causes an upward shift in the consumption function.

Rising house prices may also give rise to a phenomenon known as **mortgage equity withdrawal**. As house prices rise, consumers are able to obtain loans secured on the rising values of their properties. These loans can be used to purchase a wide range of goods and services and will boost consumer expenditure.

However, if asset prices fall, consumers can be left with a **net worth problem**. That is, they have liabilities or debts that exceed the value of their assets. To eliminate this problem consumers have to repay debts by saving. Higher saving means that consumer spending will have to fall.

7. CONSUMER CONFIDENCE

Consumer confidence is strongly correlated with expenditure. When confidence is falling it is usually a reliable indicator of a fall in the growth of spending. If consumers become more pessimistic they are less likely to commit themselves to a major 'big-ticket' purchase.

INVESTMENT SPENDING

Investment is defined as spending on assets which are used repeatedly or continuously over a number of years to produce goods and services. Increased investment in capital goods by firms and government will allow greater production in future time periods.

For the nation's **stock of capital** to increase, **net investment** must be positive. This means that **gross investment** is higher than **depreciation or capital consumption**. Capital consumption, often thought of as the wear and tear on machinery, is defined as the amount of fixed capital resources used up in the process of production during the year. If total investment in the economy is greater than the amount of capital resources used up in the production process, then the nation's capital stock will grow.

KEY DEFINITIONS AND CONCEPTS

▶ **Fixed Investment** – is spending on new machinery, plant, buildings, vehicles, etc. that will be used continuously or repeatedly in a production process. This would include machinery in a factory, computers in an office and aeroplanes belonging to an airline.

▶ **Working Capital** – is spending on stocks which are held by their producers before they are sold, stocks of raw materials and work in progress. The accumulation of stocks by firms, whether voluntary or involuntary, is counted as investment.

▶ **Gross Fixed Capital Formation** (GFCF) – is expenditure on fixed assets (buildings, vehicles and plant, etc.) either for replacing or adding to the stock of fixed assets. Expenditure on maintenance and repairs is excluded.

ECONOMIC FACTORS AFFECTING INVESTMENT SPENDING

1. CHANGES IN AGGREGATE DEMAND

The **accelerator model** stresses that **investment in the economy is demand induced**. It is based on the assumption of a stable **capital to output ratio**. This is defined as the amount of capital needed to produce a given quantity of output. It is usually expressed as a ratio. If the capital to output ratio was 3:1, then a firm would need £3000 of capital to produce £1000 of output.

The **accelerator concept** can be explained with a simple example. Consider a firm with the **capacity to produce £1000** of output per week. If the current level of demand for its output is £800 per week, then the firm is unlikely to invest in new machinery because it has **spare capacity**. Suppose demand for the firm's output rises **to £1,200 per week**. The firm will not be able to meet this new level of demand because it has **insufficient capacity**. In order to produce the additional £200 of output, the firm will have to invest in new capital equipment. If the capital to output ratio is 3:1, then a firm will need £600 of capital to produce the extra £200 of output.

Investment is, therefore, seen to be a function of the rate of change of GDP or aggregate demand. In reality, a **slowdown** in the growth of demand may actually cause a fall in the demand for capital investment.

There are some criticisms of the accelerator model and these explain why a rise in aggregate demand may not always result in a rise in investment:

▶ If an increase in demand is seen as **transitory**, then a firm may not invest because it will not want to be left with idle machines in the future.

▶ A firm may be able to increase capacity without investment if it uses **overtime** or employs more staff.

▶ Firms may not have to invest if they are operating with **spare capacity** and can meet an increase in demand by using existing inputs more intensively or with greater efficiency.

2. INTEREST RATES

Most students know that higher interest rates should have a negative impact on investment. Few, however, can explain the transmission mechanisms. These are outlined below:

▶ Many firms raise finance for investment by borrowing from financial institutions. A rise in interest rates will increase the cost of financing such schemes. This means there will be a rise in the cost of investment relative to the yield and, as a result, investment projects on the margin may become unprofitable. A firm will only invest if the yield of a project exceeds the cost. The **inverse relationship** between investment and the rate of interest can be shown graphically as in Diagram 9.3.

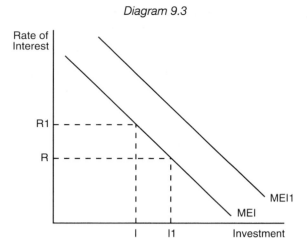

Diagram 9.3

▶ The relationship between the two variables is represented by the **marginal efficiency of investment** (MEI) curve. If a project were to yield a return of R1, but interest rates were at R this investment would be undertaken as the yield is greater than the cost. If, however, interest rates rose to R1 or above, it would now be unprofitable, as the cost of the investment would be greater than the yield. To summarise, a rise in the rate of interest leads to fall in the level of investment.

▶ A rise in the rate of interest increases the **opportunity cost** of using internal funds to finance investment projects. Some marginal investment projects may not take place as firms decide that they can attain a better rate of return by depositing their retained profits in a bank.

▶ Higher interest rates **reduce** the level of **aggregate demand**. This reduces investment via the **accelerator process**. Higher interest rates are also likely to **reduce business confidence and corporate profitability**. This applies further downward pressure on investment.

3. PROFITABILITY

A rise in the level of **corporate profitability** should have a positive impact on investment levels. A rise in profitability is usually a signal that the **rate of return** on investment projects will increase and hence more investment projects will become profitable. In Diagram 9.3, the MEI curve will shift to the right (from MEI to MEI 1) and investment will increase at each and every rate of interest. An increase in profits also allows the firm to invest using internal funds, which are usually cheaper than other forms of corporate finance.

4. BUSINESS CONFIDENCE

This has a strong positive impact on investment levels. Levels of confidence are a function of the factors that we have previously discussed.

5. CORPORATE TAXATION

A **fall in corporation tax** will **increase the post-tax rate of return** of a new investment with the result that more investment projects become viable. Tax allowances also influence the extent to which firms can afford to write off depreciating machinery and replace equipment on a regular basis.

WHY DO FIRMS INVEST?

A positive level of net investment implies a rise in the firm's **capital stock** and a long run expansion. The reasons for undertaking an investment project are varied:

▶ To take advantage of **higher expected profits** from expanding output.

▶ To generate a **rise in productive capacity** to meet increased demand.

▶ To **improve efficiency** via technological progress.

▶ To **exploit economies of scale** (see Chapter 5).

► As part of a **long run process of capital/labour substitution**; perhaps in response to changes in the relative prices of the factors of production. Higher wage costs relative to capital costs could encourage this strategy.

► As a **barrier to entry** – some investment projects give firms significant cost advantages. This may deter potential competitors from entering a market (see Chapter 6 and the section on monopoly).

THE ECONOMIC EFFECTS OF CAPITAL INVESTMENT

Changes in investment will have **short-term effects on the demand side** of the economy and more **long-term effects on the supply side** of the economy.

Diagram 9.4

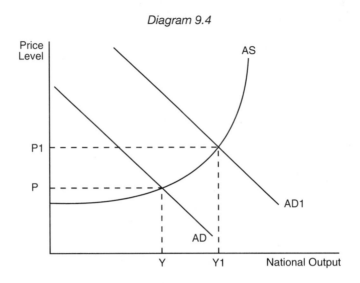

The short-term effects of a rise in investment are examined in Diagram 9.4. Investment is a component of aggregate demand and a rise in this variable will shift the aggregate demand curve to the right from AD to AD1. This will result in a rise in national output from Y to Y1, and cause **economic growth**. The rise in national output will be greater than the change in investment because of the operation of the **multiplier**. There will also be some **demand pull inflation** (see Chapter 13) as the price level has increased from P to P1.

SUPPLY SIDE EFFECTS

In the long run, a rise in net investment will increase the **productive capacity** of the economy and, if the new capital embodies new technology, it will also reduce the **costs of production**. A rise in capacity and/or a fall in costs will shift the AS curse to the right. This is illustrated in Diagram 9.5. A rise in aggregate supply will cause a rise in national output from Y1 to Y2 and a fall in the price level from P1 to P2. This will help the economy to achieve **growth without inflation**.

Diagram 9.5

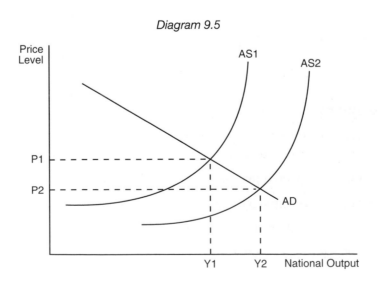

There is a strong positive correlation between investment levels and economic growth. Countries that invest a high proportion of their GDP tend to experience a higher rate of growth. Higher investment should also improve a nation's **international competitiveness**. This will help a country to expand exports of goods and services and compete more effectively against imports from other economies.

New capital machinery is likely to embody new technology. This allows firms who invest heavily to produce goods and provide services of higher quality. Spending which adds to the **stock of capital** can also create new employment in the **capital goods industries**. However, there may be a negative effect on total employment if the main driving force behind investment is to introduce **labour-saving** technology through **capital-labour substitution**.

Chapter 10
MONETARY ECONOMICS AND INTEREST RATES

Monetary policy involves the manipulation of **interest rates** and the **money supply** to influence the rate of growth of **aggregate demand and inflation**. Changes in monetary policy will also have an impact on the **exchange rate** (see Chapter 17).

THE FUNCTIONS OF MONEY

Money is any asset that is acceptable in the payment of transactions or in the settlement of debts. Money is defined by its functions. These can be summarised as follows:

1. **Medium of exchange** – money allows economic agents to exchange goods without the need for barter.

2. **Store of value** – individuals can choose to forgo consumption in the current time period and **save** to increase their spending power in the future. They are more likely to do this when money holds its value. Inflation has the effect of reducing the **internal purchasing power of money**.

3. **Unit of account** – this enables us to compare the relative prices of goods and services in pounds and pence.

4. **Standard of deferred payment** – money allows payment for goods and services consumed today in a future time period. This could include the mortgage on a house or a loan to purchase a car for example.

IS THERE A UNIQUE MEASURE OF MONEY?

There is no unique measure of money because it is used in such a wide variety of ways. The two main measures of money, **M0 and M4**, are recorded by the Bank of England.

M0 (Narrow money) – consists of Sterling notes and coins in circulation outside the Bank of England, plus the operational balances of commercial banks at the Bank of England. Over 99% of M0 is made up of notes and coins so this form of money is used mainly as a medium of exchange. It is estimated that each adult holds around £100 per week for **transactions purposes**. The operational balances held by commercial banks at the Bank of England are to ensure the liquidity of the financial system. Commercial banks currently only have to hold 0.35% of their deposits at the Bank.

M0 measures the **cash base in the economy.** Most economists see M0 as a **co-incident indicator** of consumer spending and retail sales. M0 simply reflects changes in the economic cycle, but does not cause them.

M4 (Broad money) – consists of Sterling notes and coins and all Sterling deposits held at UK financial institutions by the private sector. It includes **deposits** held by the private sector (households and firms) for transactions and savings purposes at banks and building societies. It also includes new money created by **lending** in the form of **loans** and **overdrafts.** M4 fulfils the requirements of all four functions of money.

WHAT DETERMINES THE ABILITY OF COMMERCIAL BANKS TO LEND?

The main way banks and building societies make a **profit** is by **bank lending**. The rate of interest that they charge customers to borrow is far greater than the interest that they pay on savings deposited with them. If they lend money prudently this interest rate differential allows them to make a profit. When a financial institution grants a loan to a customer, **bank liabilities and assets** rise by the same amount and so does the **broad money supply**.

It is clearly in the interest of a financial institution (bank or building society) to increase its lending, but it must maintain its **liquidity**. That is, it must hold sufficient cash to meet the daily needs of its customers. The remainder of its **cash base** can be lent out. If its cash base is decreased this reduces its ability to lend and vice versa. The amount of money banks can lend to their customers is also determined by the **credit multiplier**. This is defined as **1/cash ratio**.

Suppose a bank decides that it has to hold **20%** of its cash to meet the daily needs of its customers. The **bank's**

cash ratio would be 0.2 and the **credit multiplier** (1/0.2) would be equal to **5**. This means that the bank can support deposits (which include bank lending) up to five times the size of its cash base. **Thus, if the bank receives a £100 cash deposit this allows it make up to £400 of loans over a period of time and support total deposits of £500.** This assumes that there is a demand for credit and that all loans are spent and returned to the banking system. Rather like the national income multiplier (see Chapter 8) the process is not instantaneous and it takes some time before bank lending can rise by the full amount. If the **cash ratio increases**, or if there is a **fall in the cash base** then the bank's **ability to lend is reduced**.

CAN THE BANK OF ENGLAND REDUCE THE ABILITY OF COMMERCIAL BANKS TO LEND?

The Bank of England can choose to implement policies to control the amount that financial institutions lend. If the Central Bank directly **limits the amount of bank lending** it can **reduce the growth in broad money**. Policies to control the growth of bank lending and the money supply were used in the early 1980s without a great deal of success. Today, there are **no supply side controls on the growth of bank lending** and the Bank of **England no longer targets the rate of growth of the money supply** (M0 or M4).

The focus of UK monetary policy has changed. The Bank of England now attempts to influence **the demand for credit via changes in the rate of interest**. A rise in interest rates will increase the cost of borrowing, encourage saving and reduce the demand for bank lending. This should reduce the rate of growth of broad money and also the level of aggregate demand. The main problem with using this approach is that the demand for credit is **interest inelastic**. It **takes time** for changes in interest rates to have a noticeable effect on the total level of demand in the economy.

INTEREST RATES

There is no unique rate of interest in an economy. Anyone who browses through a financial newspaper will see that there are literally hundreds of different interest rates available. In general, interest rates measure the **rate of return on savings** and the **cost of borrowed money**. All rates tend to move in the same direction and can have a large effect on the economy as a whole, as well as on individual markets and industries.

MAIN INTEREST RATES

1. Base interest rates (now set by the Bank of England).
2. Repo rate – the rate at which the Bank of England lends to the money market.
3. Interest rate on long-term Government bonds (e.g. the ten year or twenty year long bond yield).
4. Mortgage interest rates for homeowners (options include variable and fixed rate loans).
5. Savings rates on specific Bank and Building Society Accounts.
6. The real rate of interest (the rate of interest adjusted for the rate of inflation).
7. The net real rate of interest is the rate of interest on savings after taking into account inflation and taxation of interest.

INTEREST RATE DETERMINATION

Two theories have been developed to explain interest rate determination. Both believe that the **interest rate**, like any other price, is determined by the interaction of **demand and supply**.

Classical economists believe that the **demand and supply of loanable funds** determines interest rates. **Demand for loanable funds** comes from **businesses and households**. Businesses will demand funds for investment projects and households will demand loans for mortgages and consumer durables. **The demand for loanable funds is a downward sloping curve**, as there is a higher demand for funds at lower rate of interest.

The **supply of loanable funds** is determined by the level of **saving** in the economy. It is an **upward sloping curve** as there will be a positive relationship between savings and interest rates. The interest rate is determined by the interaction of demand and supply. If demand shifts to the right interest rates will rise, but if supply shifts outwards there will be a fall in interest rates.

The main problem with this model is that **savers and borrowers do not always respond to changes in**

interest rates. There are many other factors that determine the demand and supply of money. Keynes developed an alternative model of interest rate determination.

KEYNESIAN LIQUIDITY PREFERENCE THEORY

Keynes believed that interest rates were determined by the **interaction of money demand and money supply**. In this way, his theory was no different to that of the classical economists. He believed, however, that the demand for money was determined by three different factors:

TRANSACTIONS DEMAND – this is money used for the purchase of goods and services. The transactions demand for money is positively related to real incomes and inflation. As an individual's income rises, or as prices in the shops increase, they will have to hold more cash to carry out their everyday transactions.

PRECAUTIONARY BALANCES – this is money held to cover unexpected items of expenditure. As with the transactions demand for money, it is positively correlated with real incomes and inflation. Neither the transactions or speculative demand for money is influenced by the rate of interest. They are both **interest inelastic**.

SPECULATIVE BALANCES – this is money that is not held for transaction purposes but in place of other financial assets, usually because they are expected to fall in price. Keynes demonstrated that there was an inverse relationship between the price of a bond and the rate of interest. For example, suppose a bond is issued for £100 and its annual return (coupon) is £20. The annual rate of interest is 20%. If the market rate of interest now falls to 10% the price of the bond will increase to £200. The rationale behind this is that, in order to secure the same return of £20 in any other financial asset, £200 would have to be invested. Conversely, if the rate of interest increases, the price of bonds will fall.

Keynes argued that each individual has a view about an 'average' rate of interest. If the current rate was above the average rate then a rational individual would expect interest rates to fall. Similarly, if current rates are below the average rate then obviously interest rates would be expected to rise.

▶ At high rates of interest, individuals expect interest rates to fall and bond prices to rise. To benefit from the rise in bond prices individuals use their speculative balances to buy bonds. So, when interest rates are high, speculative balances are low.

▶ At low rates of interest, individuals expect interest rates to rise and bond prices to fall. To avoid the capital losses associated with a fall in the price of bonds individuals will sell their bonds and add to their speculative cash balances. Thus, when interest rates are low, speculative balances will be high.

There is an inverse relationship between the rate of interest and the speculative demand for money.

The total **demand for money** is obtained by summating the transactions, precautionary and speculative demand for money. Represented graphically, it is sometimes called the **liquidity preference curve** and is inversely related to the rate of interest. The liquidity preference curve is shown in Diagram 10.1, and is labelled Md.

THE MONEY SUPPLY AND MONEY DEMAND TOGETHER

The supply of money is the **stock of liquid assets** in an economy that can be exchanged for goods and services. In theory it is assumed that the money supply is fixed and is determined by the Central Bank. The total demand for money and the money supply can be combined to determine the market rate of interest. This is illustrated in Diagram 10.1.

▶ Interest rates are determined by the interaction of money demand (Md) and money supply (Ms) and are initially set at the equilibrium level R.

▶ An increase in the money supply from Ms to Ms1 will result in a fall in interest rates to R1.

▶ An increase in the demand for money from Md to Md1 causes a rise in interest rates to R2. The rise in money demand could have been caused by either an increase in real incomes or by a rise in the price level.

Diagram 10.1

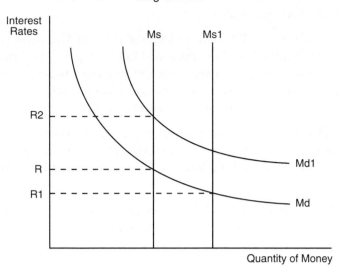

THE REALITY OF INTEREST RATE DETERMINATION

In reality, interest rates are set by the **Bank of England** (BOE). It is important to understand how the BOE influences interest rates via its daily intervention in the London **money markets**.

The BOE deals with a small group of traders who are active in the money market. This group includes banks, building societies and security dealers. Normally this group of traders has to **borrow money** from the BOE, as there is a shortage of liquidity in the money market each day. The BOE is the **sole provider of liquidity** and will provide finance at its official '**repo rate**'. This is short for **sale and repurchase agreement**. The repo rate at which the BOE lends to the traders is quickly passed on, influencing interest rates in the whole economy. For example, the rate of interest charged on mortgages and the rates of interest on offer to savers.

HOW ARE INTEREST RATES CHANGED?

The 1988 Bank of England Act gives the BOE operational responsibility for setting interest rates to meet the Government's inflation target. The current inflation target is to achieve **underlying inflation**, measured by the **RPIX**, of **2.5%** (this is explained in more detail in Chapter 13). If the underlying rate of inflation rises above 3.5%, or falls below 1.5%, the Governor of the Bank of England must write an open letter to the Chancellor to explain the reasons why the target has not been met.

Each month the **Monetary Policy Committee** (MPC) meets to decide what should happen to the level of interest rates. The MPC has **nine members** including the Governor of the Bank of England and four external economists appointed by the Chancellor. The **repo rate** that the BOE sets in the money market only changes when the MPC decides that a change in interest rates is necessary. The MPC studies the **economic news and data** that has emerged over the course of the month. They consider all factors that will have an influence on inflation over the **next two years**. When they have assessed the current state of the economy there is a vote on the final decision of interest rates. Because of the **time lags** involved between a change in interest rates and their final effect on inflation, rates need to change as a **pre-emptive strike** against inflation.

WHAT FACTORS MAY CAUSE A RISE IN INTEREST RATES?

1. **INFLATION TARGET** – If inflation approaches or exceeds the 2.5% target, it is likely that the MPC **will raise interest rates** to **reduce inflationary pressure**.

2. **MONEY SUPPLY** – **Rapid growth in M0 and M4** is often a sign that consumer demand and borrowing is increasing too quickly. Higher interest rates may be required to increase saving and to curb the demand for new loans. This will reduce consumer expenditure and **demand pull inflation** (see Chapter 13).

3. **ASSET PRICES** – the **rapid growth of asset prices**, particularly **house prices**, leads to positive **wealth effects**. Rising consumer confidence and increased mortgage equity withdrawal may boost consumer

expenditure and create demand pull inflation. Higher interest rates should reduce confidence and slow the growth in consumer spending and inflation.

4. **EXCHANGE RATE** – a **fall in Sterling** will reduce the price of UK exports, while making imported goods more expensive. The resulting rise in exports and fall in imports will **increase aggregate demand** and create inflationary pressure. The increased price of imported products will also create **cost push inflation** (see Chapter 13). A rise in interest rates is likely to lead to an **inflow of 'hot money'** from overseas investors. This should increase the value of Sterling and reduce the inflationary effects described above.

5. **ECONOMIC GROWTH** – if **real GDP** grows beyond its **long run trend**, the **output gap** (the difference between actual and potential output) will close. As the AD curve shifts to the right the economy will move closer to full employment. Demand pull inflation is likely to rise and the MPC may choose to raise interest rates.

6. **COMMODITY PRICES** – a rise in the price of commodities, such as oil, aluminium or coffee, will increase firms' costs and add to **cost push** inflationary pressure.

7. **LABOUR MARKET** – Falling unemployment and skill shortages will force up wages and earnings. This will create **wage inflation** as firms' costs are pushed up. Higher interest rates should reduce aggregate demand and, as a result, the demand for labour will fall. This should reduce the rate of growth in wages and cost push inflationary pressure.

EFFECTS OF INTEREST RATE CHANGES ON THE ECONOMY

A change in interest rates can have wide-ranging effects on the economy. When answering exam questions, it is important to explain the '**transmission mechanisms**'. That is how a change in interest rates affects an economic variable. By looking at the relevant chapters you should be able to explain the impact of a change in interest rates on:

- consumer confidence
- consumption
- economic growth
- exports and imports
- inflation
- investment
- the current account of the balance of payments
- the exchange rate
- the housing market
- unemployment

It is also important to be able to highlight the **time lags** that exist between a change in interest rates and the final effect on output, employment and prices. It can take between 12 and 18 months for the full effect of an interest rate change to impact on the economy.

Chapter 11
FISCAL POLICY

Fiscal policy involves the use of **government expenditure and taxation** to influence the level and composition of **aggregate demand**. A rise in government expenditure, or a fall in taxation, should increase aggregate demand and boost employment.

GOVERNMENT EXPENDITURE

KEY DEFINITIONS

▶ **General government expenditure** – consists of the combined **capital** and **current spending** of central and local government including debt interest.

▶ **General government final consumption** – is central government and local government spending on **goods and services**. It also includes spending on **public sector employment**, but excludes **transfer payments**.

▶ **Transfer payments** are money transfers from the government to benefit recipients for which **no output is produced**. Good examples include pensions, income support and job seeker's allowance. Transfer payments are paid through the operation of the **social security system.**

WHY DO WE NEED GOVERNMENT EXPENDITURE?

1. Public and merit goods

Public goods **would not be provided by the private sector**. Plans to build schemes, such as street lighting and flood control systems, would not take place because it would be impossible for a private firm to charge consumers for the good or service. This is because these products are **non-excludable**, i.e. they cannot be confined to those who have paid for them. This clearly creates a need for the **state provision** of public goods. A more detailed explanation of public goods and merit goods is undertaken in Chapter 7.

Merit goods would be provided by the private sector in a free market, but they would be **under produced**. This is because the social benefits of services, such as education and health, exceed the private benefits. If the government wishes to increase production, and move towards the **socially optimal level of production,** it will have to subsidise or provide some services for free. Higher spending on these merit goods should yield a positive **social rate of return** and lead to an improvement in total **economic welfare**.

2. The redistribution of income and wealth

Many economists believe that the government should try and achieve a **more equal distribution of income**. Indeed one of the aims of the social security system is to carry out the **redistribution of income** and to reduce **income inequalities.** It does this by providing a basic **minimum level of income** for those out of work and providing income support for those who are on low incomes. Indeed, in the financial year 2002/3 the government will spend over £115bn on the social security system. **Progressive income taxes** also have the effect of diminishing the gap between those on low and high incomes. This is explained later in the Chapter.

3. Regulation of economic activities

The government intervenes via **enforcement agencies** to ensure that economic activities **do not adversely affect the public interest**. It is taken for granted that our workplace is safe and that the water we drink is not polluted, but without Health and Safety inspections and the work of the Environment Agency these minimum standards could not be guaranteed. The cost of protecting the public interest is substantial and has grown in recent years with the expansion in the number of regulatory bodies. Many new regulators have been set up to monitor the performance of the privatised industries, such as the railways, water and electricity.

4. Influencing resource allocation and industrial efficiency

There are significant economic disparities in the UK and the government uses regional policies in an attempt to narrow income inequalities between regions. This is done by attracting new industries to deprived areas with high unemployment. The government offers tax breaks and grants to firms who are locating in such areas. The Department of Trade & Industry attempts to increase the efficiency and competitiveness of UK firms by offering them advice and support.

5. Influencing the level of economic activity

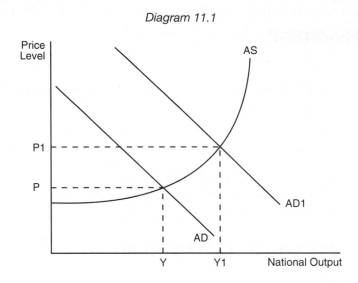

Diagram 11.1

Government expenditure is a component of aggregate demand. A rise in government spending will shift the AD curve to the right. This is illustrated in Diagram 11.1. The rise in aggregate demand will stimulate **economic growth** as national output has increased from Y to Y1. There will also be some **demand pull inflation** (see Chapter 13) as the price level has increased from P to P1. The rise in prices will be greater the closer the economy is to full employment. It is important to remember that the final change in national output will be greater than the initial change in government expenditure because of the operation of the **multiplier process**.

Some increases in government expenditure may also lead to an increase in **aggregate supply**. For example, expenditure on education and training will improve the productivity of labour (output per person per hour) and raise the productive potential of the economy. This will allow the economy to achieve **higher economic growth without inflation**.

TAXATION

A tax is any **compulsory transfer** from a private individual, institution or group to central or local government.

WHY DO WE NEED TO PAY TAXES?

▶ To raise **revenue** for central and local government so they can pay for their expenditure.

▶ To influence the level of **economic activity**.

▶ Taxes can be changed to achieve more **equality** in income and wealth between households.

▶ Taxes can be used to help correct for **externalities** (see Chapter 7).

▶ Import taxes may **control import volumes** and therefore improve the current account of the balance of payments (see Chapter 16).

GOVERNMENT'S OBJECTIVES FOR THE TAX SYSTEM

Broadly speaking, a government's objectives for the tax system are as follows:

▶ to keep the overall **burden of taxation** as low as possible. The tax burden is the proportion of national income taken in taxes.

▶ to reduce tax rates on income and profits to **sharpen incentives** to work and invest in the economy. It is hoped that this strategy will **boost the productive potential** of the economy and shift the AS curve outwards.

▶ to maintain a **broad tax base**. Having a range of taxes on income, wealth, profit and expenditure helps keep each separate tax rate low.

▶ to **shift the balance of taxation** away from taxes on income towards taxes on spending.

▶ to ensure taxes are applied **equally and fairly** to everyone.

▶ to use taxes to correct for **market failure** (see Chapter 7). This means **making polluters pay** for the external costs that they create.

DIRECT AND INDIRECT TAXES

We make a distinction between **direct** and **indirect taxes** although in reality the difference between these two types of taxes is not always clear cut. It is generally assumed that **direct taxation is levied on income, wealth and profit** while **indirect taxation is levied on expenditure**.

▶ **Direct taxes** include income tax, national insurance contributions, capital gains tax, council tax and corporation tax.

▶ **Indirect taxes** include VAT, excise duties on fuel and alcohol, car tax, and the TV licence.

PROGRESSIVE AND REGRESSIVE TAXES

▶ Generally, indirect taxes are seen as **regressive.** A tax is regressive when **the proportion of income paid in tax decreases as income rises**.

A good example of this is the tax on cigarettes. Consider two smokers who both smoke 20 cigarettes a week. If the tax on a packet of cigarettes is £3 they will both pay the same amount of tax per week to the government. However, if one smoker earns £100 a week and the other earns £1000, they will pay a different proportion of their income in tax. The low-income smoker will pay 3% of their income (3/100 x 100), while the high-income smoker will pay 0.3% (3/1000 x 100). It is clear that the high-income smoker pays a lower proportion of their income in tax than the low-income smoker. A regressive tax therefore **widens the distribution of income** which is seen by many as being undesirable.

▶ Direct taxes, such as income tax, are **progressive** because the proportion of income paid in tax increases as income rises.

With a progressive tax, the **marginal rate of tax** (the tax rate paid on the last pound of income) exceeds the **average rate of tax** (total tax paid divided by gross income). Income earners in the UK receive a tax-free allowance and **then** the marginal rate of income tax increases with income. In 2002/3, the starting rate of tax was 10%; the basic rate then increased to 22%, whilst the final top rate for high-income earners was 40%. As a result, progressive taxes act to reduce inequalities in the distribution of income. The **post-tax distribution of income** will be less dispersed than the **pre-tax distribution**.

▶ Any tax that does not vary with income is called a **lump sum tax**. A good example of this is the TV licence.

THE EFFECTS OF TAX CHANGES ON THE ECONOMY

Taxation affects both the **demand side** and the **supply-side** of the economy. Consider the demand side effects of the following tax changes:

▶ A rise in **income tax**, or **national insurance contributions**, will reduce the **real disposable incomes** of those in work. This should **reduce consumer spending** in the economy and the level of aggregate demand.

▶ A rise in **corporation tax** (a tax on company profits) will reduce the level of post-tax profits. This will reduce the **post-tax rate of return** on investment projects and, as a result, fewer investment projects will be profitable. This will shift the marginal efficiency of investment (MEI) curve inwards, and **decrease investment** at each and every rate of interest (see Chapter 9). The fall in investment will reduce the level of aggregate demand in the economy.

▶ A rise in **VAT**, or excise duties, will **increase the price** of goods and services. This should **reduce** the level of **consumer spending** in the economy. The magnitude of the fall in aggregate demand will be determined by the **price elasticity of demand** of the products affected (see Chapter 3).

The effects of a fall in aggregate demand are illustrated in Diagram 11.2.

Diagram 11.2

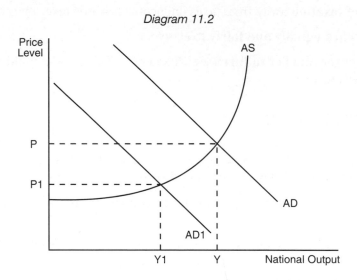

The rise in taxes shifts the aggregate demand curve left from AD to AD1. National output falls from Y to Y1 and there is also a drop in the price level from P to P1. This means that both **economic growth** and **inflation** are reduced. The fall in prices will improve the **international competitiveness** of UK goods and services. The **current account** balance will improve as the demand for exports rises and the demand for imports falls (see Chapter 16).

Now we can consider the **supply side** effects of the same tax changes:

▶ A rise in **income tax rates** will have an effect on the **microeconomic** workings of the labour market. Higher income taxes will **reduce the post-tax income** of those in work. This might encourage the labour force to work more hours to maintain their income. If this increase in the number of hours worked materialised then the AS curve would shift to the right.

▶ Many economists, however, believe that a rise in income tax will **reduce the incentive to work**. It is argued that workers will substitute leisure time for work following a tax increase because the reward for working additional hours is reduced. If workers choose more leisure time, then the productive potential of the economy will drop and the AS curve will shift inwards. Indeed, many of the income tax cuts in the 1980s were fuelled by the belief that cuts in income tax would boost the supply side of the economy. This is clearly a contentious area, and the overall effects are not clear-cut, but it can be argued that a rise in income tax might shift the AS curve to the left.

▶ A rise in **corporation tax** will reduce investment. In the long run, this might reduce the **productive capacity** of the economy and shift the AS curve to the left.

▶ A rise in **VAT** increases the price of goods and services. This will result in a rise in firms' costs and will mean that they can produce less at each and every price level. The AS curve will shift to the left.

The effects of a fall in aggregate supply are illustrated in Diagram 11.3.

The fall in aggregate supply has reduced national output (Y to Y1) and increased the price level (P to P1). As a result, there is a fall in **economic growth**, and a rise in the rate of **inflation**. The rise in prices will reduce the **international competitiveness** of UK goods and services. The current account balance will deteriorate, as the demand for exports will fall, and import penetration will increase (see Chapter 16).

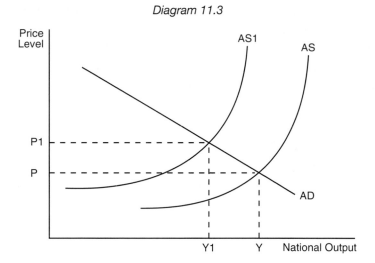

Diagram 11.3

OTHER EFFECTS OF TAXES

▶ **Foreign Direct Investment (FDI)** – Overseas companies may choose to locate some production plants in the UK if our corporate taxes are lower than those in other countries. Lower corporate taxes will increase post-tax profits and make FDI more profitable.

▶ **Employment** – taxes on employing labour, such as national insurance contributions, will increase the marginal cost of taking on additional workers. This may reduce the demand for labour and cause **unemployment**.

THE CASE FOR AND AGAINST INDIRECT TAXATION

THE CASE FOR	THE CASE AGAINST
• Changes in indirect taxes are effective in changing the pattern of demand for particular goods and services. Indirect taxes will reduce the demand for negative externalities, and output will move towards the **social optimum**.	• Indirect taxes will increase the price of goods and services. This will increase firms' costs and cause **cost-push inflation** (see Chapter 13).
• Indirect taxes **will not distort the choice between work and leisure**. As we have seen, higher direct taxes may encourage workers to reduce their hours of work and this will have a **detrimental effect on the supply-side** of the economy.	• **Revenue streams are particularly volatile.** In a boom when expenditure is high, indirect tax revenue will grow rapidly. Conversely, in a recession when expenditure falls sharply, so will the revenue stream. Indirect taxes **can be changed more easily** than direct taxes.
• Indirect taxes are **difficult to avoid**. Some workers can evade paying direct taxes by trading in cash and not declaring their income.	• Many indirect taxes have **regressive effects** and will, therefore, widen the distribution of income.
• Indirect taxes are a tax on expenditure. They may provide an **incentive to save** because saving is a way of avoiding the tax.	

GREEN TAXES

In recent years there has been a rise in the number of '**green taxes**' that the Government has introduced. These taxes penalise environmentally damaging activities. Chapter 7 provides the background and rationale for these taxes. Examples of green taxes include:

- **Lower taxes on unleaded petrol and liquid petroleum gas** (LPG). Vehicle use increases airborne pollution and contributes to global warming. By setting lower taxes on unleaded petrol and LPG, motorists are encouraged to switch away from lead based fuels. This should reduce the damage to the environment.

- The **landfill tax** increases the cost of waste disposal and encourages the recycling of resources. If the amount of refuse that society creates is reduced, there will be less damage to green field sites and the countryside.

THE PUBLIC SECTOR NET CASH REQUIREMENT

The **Public Sector Net Cash Requirement (PSNCR)** is the **combined financial deficit** of central government, local government and public corporations. In simple terms, it means that **public expenditure exceeds tax revenue**. A PSNCR is also known as a **budget deficit**. When the government is running a budget deficit it has to **borrow**. It does this through the issue of **government debt**.

The PSNCR is often confused with the **national debt**. The national debt is the total amount of borrowing undertaken by central government that has not yet been repaid. In other words, the PSNCR is the government's borrowing for just one year whilst the national debt is the sum of all outstanding government debt that has accrued over many years.

MEASURING THE PSNCR

The amount that the government has to borrow each financial year can be measured in a number of ways:

- the **nominal PSNCR –** is the total borrowing requirement in money terms.

- the **PSNCR as a % of GDP** gives economists a good measure of the **scale** of the debt problem that may exist.

- the **cyclically adjusted PSNCR** takes into account the effect the economic cycle can have on the PSNCR. For example, in a recession the PSNCR nearly always rises because of higher benefit payments and reduced tax revenues. This is an example of the operation of **automatic stabilisers**. This is explained later in this Chapter.

DOES A LARGE PSNCR MATTER?

Most economists would argue that a persistently large budget deficit can be a major problem for the government and the economy. This is because:

- a PSNCR has to be **financed**. This is done by issuing **government debt** to domestic or overseas investors. In some circumstances, interest rates may have to be raised to attract investors to buy the debt. Higher interest rates will **reduce economic growth and create unemployment**. In today's international money markets, where money flows freely between countries, it much easier to fund a budget deficit and it is not often necessary to raise interest rates.

- in the **long-run,** a high PSNCR adds to the accumulated **National Debt**. This means that the Government has to pay more each year in **debt interest charges**. The **opportunity cost** of debt interest is that the money could be used in more productive ways, such as spending on education or health. Debt interest also represents a **transfer of income** from tax payers to those who hold government debt. A high PSNCR may, therefore, cause a redistribution of income and wealth in the economy.

- 'Today's borrowing is tomorrow's taxes'. At some point in the future a budget deficit has to be reduced. The government could cut back on spending, but normally it chooses to increase **taxes**.

WHY A PSNCR IS NOT A PROBLEM

A budget deficit may not be a problem in certain circumstances. It is vital to distinguish whether the cause of the deficit is **cyclical or structural.**

- Keynesian economists argue that a PSNCR is a vital **stimulus to demand** when the economy is in a recession. A budget deficit automatically increases in a recession. This is because higher unemployment stimulates benefit expenditure and, at the same time, tax revenues fall due to lower consumer spending and shrinking incomes. These changes help **stabilise** the economy and **reduce the magnitude** of the recession.

▶ If a PSNCR is used to finance **capital spending** it may improve the performance of the economy in the long run. Spending on new infrastructure **increases the productive potential** of the economy and shifts the AS curve to the right. This may allow the economy to achieve a faster rate of growth in the future and this will generate higher tax revenues to pay for the borrowing. The current government believes that public sector borrowing should only be used to finance capital projects. This is known as the '**golden rule**' and implies that a budget deficit should never be used to fund welfare spending. This ensures that the PSNCR never spirals out of control and that borrowing always boosts the **supply side capacity** of the economy.

THE OPERATION OF FISCAL POLICY

It is important to distinguish between **automatic stabilisers** and the use of **discretionary** fiscal policy:

▶ **Automatic stabilisers** describe how government expenditure and tax revenues respond to changes in the economic cycle. There is no deliberate change in policy, but the amount of money the government spends and receives will fluctuate with the economic cycle. For example, as we have seen above, when the economy moves into recession there will be a rise in government spending (transfer payments) and a fall in tax revenues which would reduce the impact of an economic slowdown.

▶ **Discretionary** or **active fiscal policy** refers to the deliberate manipulation of government expenditure levels and tax rates.

WHAT ARE THE PROBLEMS WITH USING FISCAL POLICY?

If the government wishes to increase aggregate demand in the economy it may cut taxes and/or increase government expenditure. In theory, fiscal policy can be used to help **fine-tune** the economy so that the government can achieve its economic objectives. The reality of the situation is far more complex and there are a number of problems that might reduce the effectiveness of fiscal policy:

TIME LAGS

Fiscal policy will not instantaneously resolve a problem, such as inflation or unemployment. This is because:

▶ it takes time to recognise that aggregate demand is growing either too quickly or too slowly.

▶ it then takes time to implement an appropriate policy.

▶ it takes time for the policy to work, as the multiplier process is not immediate.

THE RELEVANCE OF THE MULTIPLIER

Suppose a government wants to increase national output by £1000m to reduce unemployment. The government cannot calculate the increase in expenditure needed without knowing the exact value of the multiplier. Suppose the multiplier is estimated to be 2, the government would increase spending by £500m. If, however, this estimate was wrong and the multiplier was 3, national output would increase by £1,500m and an inflation problem might be created. The multiplier is changing all the time as withdrawals in the economy fluctuate and, as a result, fiscal policy may not always achieve its desired goal. This makes it very difficult to **control** and **fine-tune** the economy.

CROWDING OUT

If the government attempts to stimulate the economy by reducing taxation, or increasing government spending, this might result in a **budget deficit**. To finance the deficit the government will have to **sell debt** to the private sector. In order to attract individuals and institutions to purchase the debt the government may have to **increase interest rates**. This rise in interest rates may **reduce private investment and consumption**. This is known as '**crowding out**' as some of the fiscal stimulus will be offset by the fall in consumer expenditure and investment. This will reduce the effectiveness of fiscal policy.

Chapter 12
ECONOMIC GROWTH

Economic growth is the increase in **real GDP** or **GNI** over a given period of time, usually a year. This figure is expressed as a **percentage**. For example, if real GDP increased from £100m to £104m over the course of a year, the rate of economic growth would be 4%.

REAL GDP AND THE TRADE CYCLE

National output does not rise or fall at a uniform rate. Annual and quarterly movements in real output are tracked to measure the **cyclical movement** of the economy. The economy experiences regular **trade or business cycles**. The real GDP of the UK economy from 1988 to 2001 is shown in the chart below.

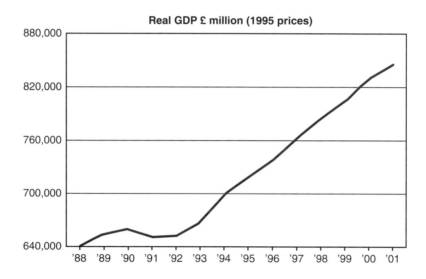

Real GDP £ million (1995 prices)

The **trend**, or average, rate of growth in the economy over the last 25 years has been around 2.5%. The different stages of the trade cycle do not have clear-cut definitions. For example, when real GDP is rising quickly above the trend rate of growth, the economy might be said to be experiencing a **boom**. American economists define a **recession** as two consecutive quarters of negative growth. The last time output fell in the UK economy was 1991 and since then the British economy has experienced its longest sustained period of economic growth.

ACTUAL AND POTENTIAL GROWTH

Economists break down growth into two forms:

▶ **Actual growth** is caused by an increase in **aggregate demand**. This concept can be linked back to **production possibility frontiers** (PPF) in Chapter 1. If an economy is operating inside its PPF, and there are unemployed resources, an increase in aggregate demand will move the economy closer to its PPF.

▶ **Potential growth** is caused by an increase in **aggregate supply**. This will shift the PPF outwards as the productive potential of the economy has increased.

WHY MIGHT ONE COUNTRY GROW FASTER THAN ANOTHER?

Consider two countries, the USA and the UK. The USA will be able to grow more quickly if its **aggregate demand** and **aggregate supply** increase at a faster rate than the UK.

Assuming both countries start from the same position, Diagram 12.1 shows the effect of the USA experiencing a faster acceleration in aggregate demand than the UK. The USA will attain a higher level of national output and **economic growth**, but also experience a higher rate of **inflation**.

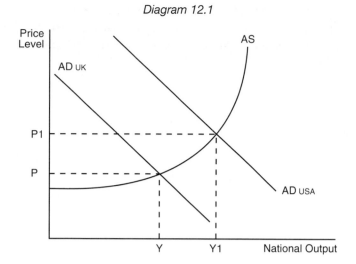

Diagram 12.1

The main reasons why the USA may experience a faster acceleration in aggregate demand are:

▶ **Higher real incomes** – may boost consumer expenditure.

▶ **Lower interest rates** – may stimulate consumption and investment.

▶ **Lower tax rates** – lower income tax and corporation tax rates will boost consumption and investment respectively.

▶ **Higher government expenditure** – this will boost AD because it is one of its components.

▶ A **lower exchange rate** – will boost exports and reduce imports.

▶ **Falling unemployment** – will raise confidence and reduce the level of **precautionary saving**.

▶ Higher levels of **borrowing**.

▶ **Rising wealth** – could trigger higher consumer spending.

POTENTIAL GROWTH

Potential economic growth comes from increasing the **quantity** and **efficiency** of the factors of production in the economy. If the USA is more successful in achieving this than the UK it will grow at a faster rate in the long term. This is illustrated in Diagram 12.2.

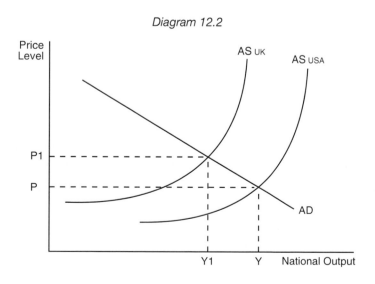

Diagram 12.2

Assuming both countries start from the same position, if the USA experiences a faster acceleration in aggregate supply it will not only attain a higher level of national output and **economic growth**, but it will also experience a lower rate of **inflation**.

The **output gap** measures the difference between the **productive potential** of the economy and the level of **actual output**. If potential growth increases at a faster rate than actual growth, the output gap will increase. This will reduce demand pull inflationary pressure (see Chapter 13) and mean that the economy is more likely to **achieve growth without inflation**.

The USA's aggregate supply might have increased at a faster rate than the UK's aggregate supply for a number of reasons:

NATURAL RESOURCES

The USA may have used its endowments of natural resources more effectively then the UK. Exploitation of natural resources; such as oil, gas, forestry, fishing and precious metals, is one pathway to economic growth. A country's natural resources will play a large role in determining its productive potential.

LABOUR RESOURCES

Labour is an important source of supply side growth. An increasing population will boost the total supply of goods and services in an economy. One problem for developed countries is that their population is relatively static. The USA may have experienced a faster rise in its **active workforce** and **labour productivity** than the UK, and this may explain why its aggregate supply has expanded more rapidly.

The size of the **active workforce** can be increased by:

▶ promoting female participation.

▶ raising retirement ages.

▶ encouraging immigration.

Income tax cuts may also encourage workers to increase their hours of work. The issues surrounding this debate were discussed in Chapter 11.

Many students confuse the terms **productivity** and **production**. Productivity is output per person per hour, or output per unit of factor of production. Production simply refers to national output.

Labour productivity may be boosted by:

▶ improving the quality of the workforce through better **education and training**.

▶ encouraging workers to increase their efforts through **performance related pay** schemes.

▶ union reforms that allow greater **labour flexibility**.

CAPITAL RESOURCES

Increasing the **capital stock** and making more efficient use of it is another crucial source of potential growth. The USA may have allocated more funds to investment than the UK. There may have also been a faster rate of technological development. This might have been stimulated by higher spending on **research and development**.

ADVANTAGES OF ECONOMIC GROWTH

1. Higher economic growth should lead to an increase in **living standards** as measured by real GDP per capita. The problems with this measure of living standards are discussed in Chapter 8.

2. The effects of growth are **cumulative**. If a country grows at 3% per annum, the economy will double in size every 24 years.

3. Economic growth should reduce **unemployment**. When output in the economy increases there should be an increase in the demand for labour. This is because labour is a **derived demand**, that is the demand for labour is dependent on the final demand for goods and services. Firms do not demand labour for its own sake.

4. Economic growth will have a positive effect on **government finances**. Economic growth will **increase tax revenues** because as output, employment and incomes rise so will the tax take. Growth will reduce

unemployment and, as a result, **expenditure on transfer payments** will fall. These two effects will combine to reduce the PSNCR. Alternatively the government could increase spending on areas such as education and health without having to put up taxes and reduce current consumption levels.

5. Rising demand and output encourages further **investment** in new capital machinery via the accelerator process (see Chapter 9). This will boost the productive capacity of the economy in the long run.

DISADVANTAGES OF ECONOMIC GROWTH

1. If actual growth exceeds potential growth there is the danger of **inflation.** The rise in prices may reduce the **international competitiveness** of the economy.

2. Economic growth will create **negative externalities,** such as increased pollution and congestion, which will damage social welfare. Those affected could experience a fall in living standards.

3. The benefits of **economic growth may not be evenly distributed**. A rise in national output may also be associated with growing inequality in society. Just because there is economic growth, it does not mean that the number of people living **below the poverty line**, i.e. in absolute poverty, will diminish.

4. Faster economic growth might lead to an **over-exploitation of scarce finite economic resources** that will limit growth prospects in the future.

MEASURING INFLATION

Inflation is the **increase in the general level of prices** over a given period of time. The most common measure of inflation in the UK is the **Retail Price Index (RPI).**

RETAIL PRICE INDEX (RPI)

▶ The RPI measures the average change in prices of a representative sample of over 670 goods and services.

▶ Each month, a market research company collects over 130,000 separate price samples. These are then used to compile the inflation statistics which measure the change in prices over the preceding 12 months.

▶ The index is **weighted** according to the proportion of income spent by the average household on categories of goods and services, such as food and housing. The weights are determined by the Expenditure and Food Survey that samples around 7000 households each year. Certain households are excluded from the survey. These include those households within the top 4% of incomes and pensioners. These groups are excluded to make the RPI more representative of the average household.

▶ The weights are amended periodically to reflect changing spending patterns in the economy. For example in 2002, frozen prawns and DVD players were added to the index. Over the last 25 years, the weightings for foreign travel and electrical goods have increased because these categories now take up a greater share of the average household budget. The table below shows how the weights have changed between 1998 and 2002.

RPI Section Weights (%)	1998	2002
Food	13.6	11.4
Catering	4.9	5.2
Alcohol	8.0	6.8
Tobacco	3.4	3.1
Housing	18.6	19.9
Fuel & Light	4.1	3.1
Household Goods	7.2	7.3
Household Services	5.2	6.0
Clothes	5.6	5.1
Personal Goods	4.0	4.3
Motoring	12.8	14.1
Fares	2.0	2.0
Leisure Goods & Services	10.6	11.7

THE UNDERLYING RATE OF INFLATION (RPIX)

Since September 1992 the Government has placed an alternative measure of inflation at the centre of its anti-inflationary strategy. The **underlying rate of inflation**, measured by the **RPIX**, was originally set a target rate of growth of between 1% and 4%. This was amended in 1997 when the Labour Government came to power.

The current inflation target is to achieve **underlying inflation** of **2.5%**. This target is examined in greater detail in Chapter 10.

The calculation of the RPIX is similar to the RPI, **but it excludes mortgage interest payments**. The reason for their exclusion is simple. In order to control aggregate demand and inflation the Bank of England will raise interest rates. This will increase mortgage interest payments and, therefore, increase the housing costs of the average household. As housing receives a significant weighting in the RPI (see the previous table), inflation will rise in the short run. It is somewhat perverse that the policy introduced to tackle inflation actually creates a greater problem in the short run. It is for this reason that some economists argue the effects of interest rates should be stripped out of the index. Excluding mortgage interest payments makes the RPIX **less volatile** than the RPI.

OTHER MEASURES OF INFLATION

► **The RPIY, or core rate of inflation**, excludes mortgage interest payments and indirect taxes. By stripping out the effect of these taxes, the Government can establish the **core** change of prices within the economy. Cynics would argue that it is just another way of reducing the headline rate.

► Countries within the **European Union** use a common measure of inflation – the **harmonised index of consumer prices** (HICP). This is meant to provide a standardised measure of inflation to aid international comparisons.

► **Input cost inflation** measures the prices paid by firms for raw materials, components and fuel. However, it does not include labour costs. These are measured separately by **Unit Labour Costs** (ULCs) which are calculated by dividing total labour costs by output – to give the labour cost per unit of output. A common misconception is that a rise in **wages** or **average earnings** immediately places upward pressure on prices. This is not necessarily true, since rising earnings may be offset by an equivalent increase in **productivity**, and ULCs will be left unchanged.

► The prices at which finished goods leave the factory is measured by the **Producer Price Index** (PPI). The PPI is also a good **leading indicator** of the RPI.

CAUSES OF INFLATION

1. DEMAND PULL INFLATION

Demand pull inflation occurs when **total demand for goods and services exceeds total supply**. This type of inflation happens when there has been **excessive growth in aggregate demand** or when **actual growth exceeds potential growth**. A good example of this was during the late 1980s with the so-called 'Lawson Boom'. Demand pull inflation is illustrated graphically in Diagram 13.1.

Diagram 13.1

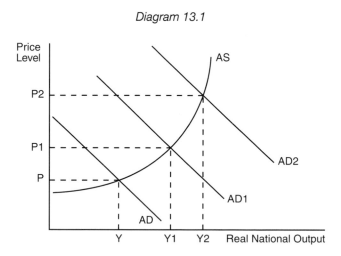

Aggregate supply (AS) shows the total supply of goods and services that firms are able to produce at each and every price level. At low levels of output when there is plenty of **spare productive capacity,** firms can easily expand output to meet increases in demand, resulting in a relatively elastic AS curve. However, as the economy

approaches full employment (or full capacity), labour and raw material shortages mean that it becomes more difficult for firms to expand production without pushing up their prices. As a result, the AS curve becomes more inelastic. When aggregate demand increases from AD to AD1 the economy is still operating at relatively low levels of capacity. There is a **large output gap** and production can expand relatively easily so firms will only implement small increases in prices from P to P1.

When aggregate demand increases from AD1 to AD2, the economy is moving towards the **full employment** of the factors of production. As the **output gap closes**, shortages of raw materials and labour mean that the firms' costs of production start to rise. At the same time, many firms will choose to widen their **profit margins**. As a result, prices will rise sharply from P1 to P2. Furthermore, it is likely that, as employment in the economy grows, demand for goods and services will become more inelastic. This will allow firms to pass on large price increases without any significant fall in demand.

2. COST PUSH INFLATION

This occurs when firms increase prices to maintain or protect profit margins after experiencing a rise in costs. The main causes are:

▶ Growth in **Unit Labour Costs** – this occurs when average wages grow faster than productivity.

▶ Rising **input costs** – such as oil, raw materials and components.

▶ Increases in **indirect taxes** – VAT and excise duties are paid by producers and will, therefore, increase their costs.

▶ Higher **import prices** – a depreciation in the currency or a rise in world inflation rates will force up import prices.

The effects of a rise in costs is illustrated in Diagram 13.2.

Diagram 13.2

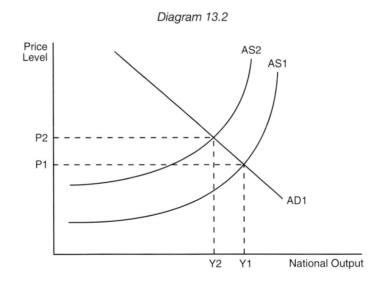

An increase in **input costs** will mean that firms can produce less at each and every price level and, as a result, the aggregate supply curve will shift to the left from AS1 to AS2.

At the new equilibrium level of national output, the economy is producing a lower level of output (Y2) at a higher price level (P2). Higher cost push inflation therefore causes a contraction in real output as well as a higher price level.

WILL AN INCREASE IN A FIRM'S COSTS ALWAYS FEED THROUGH INTO INFLATION?

No, because a firm can **absorb** an increase in costs by reducing its **profit margin**. An excellent example of this occurred after the devaluation of Sterling in September 1992. The fall in the value of the pound caused a rise in the cost of imported fuel and raw materials. Although input costs rose in 1993, this increase did not fully feed through into the prices of goods and services leaving the factory gate, as measured by Producer

Prices. Firms were forced to reduce profit margins and absorb the increase in costs or face a loss in market share. This was due to the high level of spare capacity in the economy. Effectively, firms were facing **elastic demand curves** (see Chapter 3) and any increases in price would have resulted in a fall in demand and total revenue.

3. MONETARY INFLATION

The Monetarist explanation of inflation operates through the Fisher equation:

M.V = P.T

M = Money Supply   V = Velocity of Circulation

P = Price level   T = Transactions or Output

As Monetarists assume that V and T are fixed, there is a direct relationship between the growth of the money supply and inflation. The mechanisms by which **broad money growth** (see Chapter 10) might be translated into inflation are examined below:

▶ If the growth in broad money comes from higher borrowing, consumers and firms will spend this directly on goods and services. This has a direct impact on inflation by **raising aggregate demand**. The closer the economy is to full employment, the greater the impact on inflation.

▶ The increased demand for goods and services will **increase the demand for labour**. Average earnings may rise and this could contribute to **cost push inflation.**

ECONOMIC POLICIES TO CONTROL INFLATION

SHORT TERM

Short term policies basically aim to reduce the level of **aggregate demand** in the economy. In Diagram 13.1 we can see that a reduction in aggregate demand from AD2 to AD1 will reduce the price level from P2 to P1. It is important to note that a fall in aggregate demand will not always reduce inflation. If there is a **large output gap**, and the economy is on the perfectly elastic section of its AS curve, a fall in aggregate demand will have **no impact on prices**.

1. TIGHTENING OF MONETARY POLICY

By raising interest rates the Bank of England is primarily trying to reduce consumption and investment. These are two of the key components of aggregate demand.

Higher interest rates will reduce **consumption** because there will be:

▶ a **rise in saving**. This is because the opportunity cost of spending has increased.

▶ a **fall in demand for consumer durables** purchased on credit. This is because loan repayments will increase.

▶ a fall in **'effective disposable incomes'**. The rise in mortgage interest payments will reduce homeowners' ability to spend.

Investment may also fall, as the cost of borrowing funds will increase. Some investment projects on the margin will now become unprofitable, as the cost of the project will now exceed the required rate of return (see Chapter 9).

Higher interest rates could also be used to limit **monetary inflation**. A rise in real interest rates should reduce the demand for lending and therefore reduce the growth of broad money (see Chapter 10).

The **problem** in using higher interest rates to control inflation is that in the short term it may create further inflation via the effect on **housing costs**. This was discussed earlier in the Chapter. A further dilemma is that higher interest rates **increase companies' loan repayments**, a fixed cost, and this could create **cost push inflation**.

2. DEFLATIONARY FISCAL POLICY

Deflationary fiscal policies will reduce demand pull inflation at the cost of slower economic growth and higher unemployment. Some of the policies the government might adopt include:

▶ **Higher tax rates** – higher income tax and corporation tax rates will reduce consumption and investment respectively.

▶ **Lower Government expenditure** – this will reduce aggregate demand because it is one of its components.

▶ A reduction in the amount of **public sector borrowing** (PSNCR).

3. STRENGTHEN THE POUND

This could be achieved by an **increase in interest rates** or through the **purchase of Sterling** via Central Bank intervention in the foreign exchange markets.

▶ An appreciation in the pound makes exports more expensive and should **reduce the volume of exports** and aggregate demand. It also provides UK firms with an incentive to **keep costs down** to remain competitive in the world market.

▶ A stronger pound reduces import prices. This makes firms' raw materials and components cheaper; therefore **helping them control costs**. The fall in import prices may also **increase the volume of imports** and this will reduce aggregate demand.

A rise in the value of the currency **reduces** both **demand pull** and **cost push** inflationary pressure.

4. WAGE CONTROLS

Incomes policies set limits on the rate of growth of wages and have the potential to reduce cost inflation. The government has not used such a policy since the 1970s, but it does still try to influence wage growth by restricting pay rises in the public sector. By adopting such a policy the Government hopes that private sector firms will follow its restraint and, as a result, minimise cost push inflationary effects.

Wage inflation normally falls when the economy is heading into recession and unemployment starts to rise. This causes greater **job insecurity** and some workers may trade off lower pay claims for a degree of employment protection.

LONGER TERM POLICIES TO CONTROL INFLATION

5. LABOUR MARKET REFORMS

The weakening of Trade Union power, the growth of part-time and temporary working and the expansion of flexible working hours are all moves that have increased flexibility in the labour market. If this does allow firms to control their labour costs it may reduce cost push inflationary pressure.

6. SUPPLY SIDE REFORMS

These are measures to increase **aggregate supply**. If more output can be produced at a lower cost, then the economy can achieve economic growth without inflation. This is a key long term objective of government economic policy. The effects of increasing aggregate supply are shown in Diagram 13.3. The economy experiences a rise in national output from Y1 to Y2 and a fall in inflation (P1 to P2).

The following policies may shift the AS curve to the right:

▶ A **rise in investment** increases the productive potential of the economy. It may reduce firms' production costs and, in the long term, it is likely to relieve problems of excess demand.

Any measure that stimulates **productivity**, such as expenditure on **education and training** or **research and development**, lowers unit labour costs and relieves cost pressures.

De-regulation and competition – In Chapter 6, we have seen that higher levels of competition ensure that firms attempt to minimise their costs and move towards **productive efficiency**. The European Single Market has also increased competition from other countries in the EU. The resulting rivalry stops firms exploiting any domestic monopoly power they may have, and forces all firms to keep a close eye on costs and prices. Lower costs mean that firms can produce more at each and every price and this shifts the AS curve to the right.

Diagram 13.3

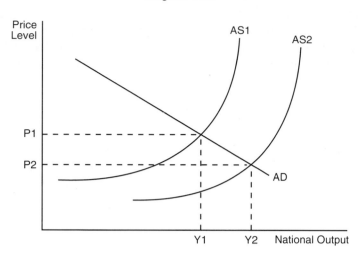

INFLATION TARGETS

Many economists believe that since the Bank of England has been given responsibility for the setting of interest rates to meet the Government's inflation target, the credibility of the UK's anti-inflationary strategy has improved. A credible and effective inflation target can have several economic benefits:

▶ It can reduce **inflationary expectations** if people believe a low inflation target will be met. This will then reflect in the **wage demands** of people in work. If employees expect low inflation they may be prepared to accept a slower growth of pay. This reduces the risk of cost-push inflation in the economy.

▶ Sustained low inflation improves prospects for higher levels of capital investment in both the manufacturing and service industries.

COSTS AND EFFECTS OF INFLATION

1. **Effect on UK competitiveness** – if the UK has higher inflation than the rest of the world it will lose competitiveness in the international market. This assumes a given exchange rate. This rise in relative inflation leads to a fall in the world share of UK exports and a rise in import penetration. See Chapter 16 on the Balance of Payments. Ultimately, this will lead to a fall in the rate of economic growth and the level of employment.

2. **The problems of a wage-price spiral** – price rises can lead to higher wage demands as workers try to maintain their standard of living. This increases firms' costs and, in an effort to maintain their profit margins, they increase prices. The process could start all over again and inflation may get out of control. Higher inflation causes an upward shift in **inflationary expectations** that are then incorporated into wage bargaining. It can take some time for these expectations to be controlled.

3. **Reduction in the real value of savings** – especially if real interest rates (interest rates – inflation) are negative. This means the rate of interest does not fully compensate for the increase in the general price level. In contrast, **borrowers** see the **real value of their debt diminish**. Inflation, therefore, favours borrowers at the expense of savers.

4. **Consumers and businesses on fixed incomes will lose out.** Many pensioners are on fixed pensions so inflation reduces the real value of their income year on year. The state pension is normally increased each year in line with the RPI so that the real value of the pension is not reduced. However it is unlikely that pensioners have the same spending patterns as those used to create the weights from which the RPI figure is calculated. This may leave them worse off.

5. Inflation usually leads to **higher interest rates**, which will reduce economic growth and employment (see Chapter 10 on Monetary Policy and the Bank of England).

6. **Disruption of business planning** – high and volatile inflation creates uncertainty about the future. This

makes planning and budgeting difficult as firms become unsure about what will happen to their costs. This could have a detrimental effect on investment in the economy. For example, if inflation is high and volatile, firms may demand a higher rate of return on investment projects before they will go ahead with the capital spending. These **hurdle rates** may cause projects to be cancelled or postponed until economic conditions improve. A low rate of capital investment clearly damages the productive potential of the economy and may reduce productivity growth.

7. Cost inflation usually leads to a slower growth of **profits** and this is likely to reduce the level of investment in the economy.

8. Inflation distorts the operation of the price mechanism and can result in an **inefficient allocation of resources.** When inflation is volatile, consumers and firms are unlikely to have sufficient information on relative price levels to make informed choices about which products to purchase and supply.

9. **Shoe leather costs** – when prices are unstable there will be an increase in search times to discover more about prices. Inflation increases the opportunity cost of holding money, so people make more visits to their banks and building societies (wearing out their shoe leather!).

10. **Menu costs** – are the extra costs to firms of changing price information.

In general, the costs of inflation to consumers are smaller when inflation is **anticipated.** Consumers can then take steps to protect **the real value** of their **income** and **savings**. The economic problems from high and variable inflation are more serious for the whole economy in the long run, particularly for those countries that are heavily dependent on international trade for their prosperity.

Chapter 14
UNEMPLOYMENT

DEFINITION OF UNEMPLOYMENT

The unemployed are those registered as **able, available and willing to work** at the **going wage rate** in any **suitable job** who cannot find employment.

Unemployment is a **stock** concept, that is it measures the number of people who are out of work at a given period of time. However, each month workers lose their jobs while others find new employment. Unemployment will fall if the flow of workers finding employment is greater than the number of workers losing their jobs.

UNEMPLOYMENT FIGURES

In April 1998, the Government introduced a new monthly Labour Force Survey of 6000 households using a different measure of unemployment. The new measure is based on the **International Labour Organisation's** (ILO) definition of unemployment. It covers those who have **looked for work in the past four weeks** and are **able to start work in the next two weeks**. The previous monthly count only included those who were **unemployed and claiming benefit** on a given day each month.

Generally the ILO level of unemployment is above the claimant count figure. This is because the claimant count excludes a number of people who are classed as unemployed under the ILO definition. The most significant group are women seeking work whose partners are employed. These women are not entitled to benefits for being unemployed if their partner's income is above a certain level and, as a result, they would not appear in the claimant count statistics.

PROBLEMS WITH THE UNEMPLOYMENT FIGURES

Over the last 20 years, the **claimant count measure** has come under increasing criticism because it is **open to manipulation by the government**. Politicians have the power to change the rules on who is entitled to claim unemployment benefits and how they set the rules can distort the figures. Since 1979, there have been over 30 changes; most of which have reduced the claimant count.

The **ILO measure** is an internationally recognised statistic, but even this method of calculation has its problems. As it is collected by surveying only 6000 households, there is a possibility that **the sample may not be truly representative**.

Both measures of unemployment may **understate** the true size of the unemployment problem because:

▶ Some workers who are unemployed are forced to take part in **training schemes**. This is not usually permanent employment and when the scheme finishes they will, once again, be classed as unemployed.

▶ Part time workers who wish to work full time are not included in the statistics. These workers are classed as **underemployed**.

▶ Some workers, particularly women with families, may not be actively seeking work, but would take a job if it were offered to them.

The figures may **overstate** the unemployment problem if workers profess to be actively seeking work, and illegally collect job seeker's allowance, when they already have a job.

SEASONAL ADJUSTMENT

The unemployment statistics are often seasonally adjusted to allow for fluctuations due solely to the time period at which the data was collected. For example, at Christmas, the unemployment figures may be artificially reduced due to the number of people taking temporary employment in the retail sector. The seasonally adjusted unemployment figures will exclude this rise in temporary employment from their calculations. In this way, it gives a clearer picture of the underlying forces that influence the level of unemployment.

MAIN CAUSES OF UNEMPLOYMENT

1. REAL WAGE UNEMPLOYMENT (CLASSICAL)

Real wage unemployment is a form of **disequilibrium unemployment** that occurs when **real wages** are forced above **the market clearing level**. Traditionally, **trade unions** and **minimum wage legislation** have been seen as the main cause of this type of unemployment.

Suppose that having initially been in equilibrium where the demand for labour was equal to the supply of labour, a minimum wage W1 is set above the market clearing wage W. The effects of such an action are illustrated in Diagram 14.1.

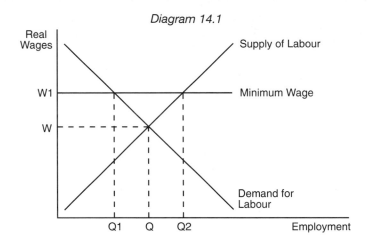

Diagram 14.1

At the new minimum wage W1, the **demand for labour** has contracted from Q to Q1 while the supply of labour has expanded from Q to Q2. Firms will tend to employ fewer workers when the **marginal cost** of employing them increases. At the same time, more workers will be willing to take jobs at higher wage rates.

At real wage W1, there is an **excess supply of labour**. The supply of labour now exceeds the demand for labour and we have disequilibrium unemployment equal to Q1-Q2.

We are assuming that a rise in real wages does not cause a rise in productivity or consumer expenditure. If productivity, and/or consumption, did increase then the demand for labour would shift to the right and the rise in unemployment would be far smaller.

POLICIES TO REDUCE REAL WAGE UNEMPLOYMENT

Most prescriptions for reducing real wage unemployment centre around the idea of making each labour market more **flexible**, so that pay conditions become more adaptable to changing demand and supply conditions. Real wages should rise when demand, output and employment are rising, but they may need to fall if an industry experiences a recession which puts jobs at threat.

What is a flexible labour market?

This is a labour market where there are:

▶ flexible employment patterns both in terms of the hours worked and the skills required of the workforce. This often involves offering short term contracts to workers in industries where labour demand is variable.

▶ flexible pay arrangements such as performance related pay (where pay is linked to profits or productivity). The increased use of regional pay awards makes the labour market more responsive to local supply and demand conditions.

In reality, labour markets in the UK are some of the **most flexible in Europe**. The power of trade unions has diminished significantly over the last 20 years. Government legislation in the 1980s abolished the legal immunity of unions and made it illegal to strike without a ballot. This has meant that, in most markets, trade unions do not have the power to adopt an aggressive stance in pay negotiations. Without any real bargaining power they find it very difficult to force wages above the market clearing level.

Reduced union power and **greater flexibility** has changed the landscape of the UK labour market. Indeed some commentators now believe that **real wage unemployment is no longer a significant cause of unemployment** in the UK. Opponents to this viewpoint say that the implementation of the minimum wage in 1999 introduced a new imperfection into the labour market.

Without the **abolition of the minimum wage** the labour market will be unable to work properly. It could, however, be argued that because the minimum wage is set at such a low level it is **non-binding**. In Diagram 14.1, if the minimum wage is set below the market clearing wage (W) it will have no effect on the labour market. With the exception of a few sectors such as the retail, hotel and catering industries, the minimum wage does not appear to place much upward pressure on wages. If this is the case it seems unlikely that it will be a major cause of unemployment in the UK.

2. DEMAND DEFICIENT UNEMPLOYMENT

Demand deficient unemployment is associated with an **economic recession**. Labour is a **derived demand** – it is not demanded for its own sake, but because of the output that it produces. A fall in the level of output will cause a drop in the demand for labour at each wage level. As aggregate demand drops, firms will lay-off workers to reduce their costs and protect profits.

Diagram 14.2

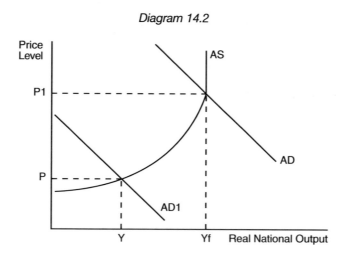

In the Diagram 14.2, the equilibrium level of national output (Y) lies below the full employment level of national output (Yf). This means that there is insufficient aggregate demand for all workers to obtain employment. The current level of demand (AD1) lies below the level required for full employment (AD).

Although demand deficient unemployment is usually associated with economic recessions it can also exist in the long run when the economy has an **output gap**. This occurs when actual output lies below potential output.

POLICIES FOR DEMAND DEFICIENT UNEMPLOYMENT

The usual government response is to raise aggregate demand. This can be achieved by utilising a variety of policy instruments.

▶ **Increase Government Expenditure** – this will boost aggregate demand because it is one of its components. The change in national output will be greater than the change in government expenditure because of the operation of the **multiplier**. The larger the value of the multiplier, the greater the effect on national output. If the government raises expenditure on infrastructure, or training, it will also boost the productive potential of the economy and shift the AS curve to the right.

▶ **Reduce Taxation** – lower income taxes will increase consumers' real disposable incomes and boost consumer expenditure.

▶ **Lower interest rates** – will encourage borrowing, reduce saving and increase consumers' real 'effective' disposable incomes. This should boost consumer expenditure and the level of aggregate demand. A drop in interest rates may also encourage firms to invest, as the cost of investment will fall.

▶ **Depreciate the pound** – this should lead to a rise in export orders for UK firms and to a fall in imports. This is because a fall in the value of the currency will reduce the price of exports and increase the cost of imports.

Remember the effects of monetary and fiscal policy are not instantaneous. It will take some time for the full effect of these policies to impact on output and employment.

3. EQUILIBRIUM UNEMPLOYMENT

Equilibrium unemployment is also sometimes referred to as the **natural rate of unemployment**. This type of unemployment can exist even when the labour market is in equilibrium. At this point the **demand for labour** equals **the supply of labour** at the going market wage rate. This is shown in Diagram 14.3. Equilibrium unemployment is the **difference between those seeking employment** and those actually **willing and able** to take a job.

Diagram 14.3

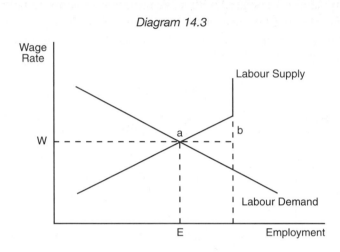

▶ The supply of labour and demand for labour are in equilibrium at wage rate (W) and employment level (E). There is still, however, some unemployment shown by the distance ab. This unemployment is caused by those workers who are unaware of vacancies, or who are unable or unwilling to find paid employment at the current wage rate (W).

▶ There are two main types of equilibrium unemployment: frictional and structural.

(a) FRICTIONAL UNEMPLOYMENT

This type of unemployment reflects **job turnover** in the labour market. Even when there are vacancies it takes people time to **search** and find a new job. During this period of time workers will remain frictionally unemployed.

Policies for frictional unemployment

▶ **Reduce Job Seeker's Allowance** – Job Seeker's Allowance replaced unemployment benefit in 1996. This new benefit, as its name suggests, has much stricter criteria regarding the search for work. The job seeker has to show that he/she is **actively seeking work** and if they are unable to prove this at fortnightly interviews they lose their benefit. This measure was introduced to reduce the level of frictional unemployment. However, if the government reduced the level of the benefit, or limited the duration of a claim, search times between jobs could be reduced even further. This is because workers would have to take a job more quickly before their financial situations deteriorated. Some economists argue that if the unemployed were financially worse off they would not be able to search for work effectively. For example, they may not be able to afford to travel to interviews or telephone potential employers.

▶ **Direct tax cuts** – the government could reduce direct taxes for the low paid to increase the post tax wage and, therefore, encourage them to find work more quickly. In April 2000, the Labour Government introduced a 10% starting rate of tax to encourage those on low incomes to reduce their search times between jobs. Most analysts believe that tax cuts on their own are insufficient to reduce frictional unemployment. The benefit system needs to be reformed to eliminate the **unemployment trap** – this is a situation where someone is financially better off not working.

▶ **Improve job information** – facilities provided by job centres, private agencies, newspapers and the Internet. The development of the Job Centre Plus programme, which provides intensive support and advice for job seekers, is one way to help workers obtain employment more quickly.

(b) STRUCTURAL UNEMPLOYMENT

This type of unemployment exists even when there are job vacancies, due to a **mismatch** between the skills of job seekers and those required by employers. People made redundant in one sector of the economy cannot immediately take up jobs in another industry, as they do not have the relevant skills. For example, it would be hard for a redundant Selby coal miner to take a job instantly in an IT based call centre. Likewise, workers laid-off from the Ebbw Vale Steel Plant in Wales may have problems in finding re-employment in the service sector. This type of unemployment is linked to the **occupational mobility of labour** – this refers to the ease with which workers can move between different types of jobs. Undoubtedly, structural unemployment is caused by the **immobility of labour**.

Structural unemployment is often centred on certain **regions** due to the long-term decline of traditional manufacturing industries, such as coal, steel, textiles and shipbuilding. Employment in these sectors contracts due to intense overseas competition and the development of new technology. **Technological unemployment** is one of the key causes of the fall in demand for labour in traditional industries. For example, the use of robotic technology in the car industry has led to a sharp decline in the number of workers employed. The scale of the **regional unemployment** problem depends on the concentration of declining industries in a specific area, the speed of fall in demand for their output and the level of labour immobility.

Policies for the structural problem

There are a number of different approaches that can be adopted to help alleviate structural unemployment. These are sometimes known as **active labour market policies**.

▶ **Regional policy** – gives grants and tax breaks to encourage firms to locate in areas of high structural unemployment. This, however, does not solve the problem of **occupational immobility**. Regional policy often demands extra retraining schemes in order to give workers the relevant skills to allow them to take up new jobs.

▶ **Investment in worker training** – The **New Deal** programme, launched in 1998, aims to provide a gateway back into employment for long-term unemployed workers. The scheme has been modified over the years and now offers opportunities to job seekers of all ages. The scheme starts with an interview to identify any gaps in a worker's skills, training or knowledge. An individual programme is then developed for each participant. The options available within the programme include:

- subsidised employment.
- work experience with employers.
- training and help with basic skills.
- a place on an environmental taskforce.

The aim of the scheme is to give workers the training and skills needed to take up jobs in their local areas. It is also hoped that real work experience will improve their **employability**.

▶ **Improving geographical mobility** – geographical mobility refers to the ease with which workers can move between different regions to attain employment. The government could provide grants or low cost housing to encourage workers to move from areas of high unemployment to regions where there are jobs. The problem with this policy is that people are inherently immobile because they are often bound by family and social ties.

▶ **The market solution** – one approach is simply to leave the problem of structural unemployment to the market. High unemployment will **drive down wages** and **new firms will be attracted into a region** to take advantage of the low costs of production. In this way the problem will eventually solve itself, but the **social deprivation created** in the short term may be considerable. Some commentators argue that intervention to solve structural unemployment slows the natural reallocation of resources to high growth areas and only makes the problem worse.

THE COSTS OF UNEMPLOYMENT

It is important to distinguish between the **economic** and **social costs** arising from high levels of unemployment.

▶ **Lost output** – unemployment causes a waste of scarce economic resources and reduces the growth potential of the economy. An economy with unemployment is producing inside its **production possibility frontier** (see Chapter 1). Unlike machinery, the hours that the unemployed do not work can never be recovered.

▶ **Impact on government expenditure, taxation and the PSNCR** – an increase in unemployment results in higher benefit payments and lower tax revenues. When individuals are unemployed, not only do they receive benefits but they pay no income tax. Because they are spending less, they contribute less to the government in indirect taxes. This rise in government spending, along with the fall in tax revenues, may result in a PSNCR.

▶ **Unemployment wastes some of the resources used in training workers**. Furthermore, workers who are unemployed for long periods become **de-skilled** as their skills become increasingly dated in a rapidly changing job market. This reduces their chances of gaining employment in the future, which in turn increases the burden on the government and the taxpayer.

▶ **Rising unemployment is linked to social and economic deprivation** – there is some relationship with crime and with social dislocation (increased divorce, worsening health and lower life expectancy). Areas of high unemployment will see falls in real incomes and an increase in income inequality.

THE UNEMPLOYMENT AND INFLATION TRADE-OFF

Economists and politicians have traditionally faced a problem of **conflicting objectives** when attempting to reduce the level of unemployment in the UK. When **unemployment falls** below a certain level it is likely that **inflation will start to accelerate**. The relationship between inflation and unemployment can be examined by looking at the **Phillips Curve** and a concept known as the **Non Accelerating Inflation Rate of Unemployment** (NAIRU). NAIRU gives an indication of the level of unemployment that can exist without upward pressure being placed on prices. There is no precise measure of NAIRU and, as a result, the point at which falling unemployment leads to inflation is uncertain. The relationship between unemployment and inflation is illustrated in Diagram 14.4.

Diagram 14.4 – The Phillips Curve

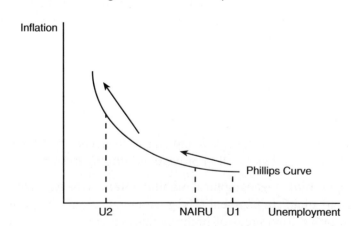

In Diagram 14.4, as unemployment falls from U1 towards NAIRU, there is a large output gap and firms can increase production by calling on a large pool of unemployed labour. There will be no increase in wages or inflation. If unemployment drops below NAIRU, skill shortages start to exert upward pressure on wages and producer prices, until any further falls in unemployment lead to higher inflation. The Phillips Curve becomes inelastic and the trade-off between unemployment and inflation worsens. This can be see as unemployment drops from NAIRU to U2.

POLICY IMPLICATIONS

The policy implications of the Phillips Curve are easily interpreted. The government can increase aggregate demand to reduce unemployment up until NAIRU and there will be no significant rise in inflation. This is because there is a large output gap and the economy is operating on the elastic section of the aggregate supply curve. If it increases aggregate demand beyond this point, then unemployment will fall but inflation will start to rise.

If the Government is committed to low inflation the likelihood of reducing unemployment much below the estimated NAIRU is minimal. The only way the government can reduce both unemployment and inflation is if it can shift the Phillips Curve inwards. This requires the implementation of policies that increase the productive potential of the economy and reduce NAIRU. This is illustrated in Diagram 14.5.

Diagram 14.5

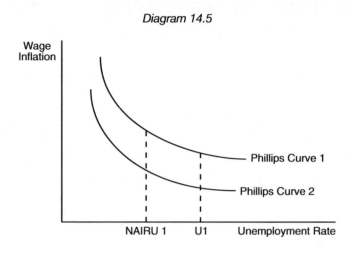

If the Phillips Curve shifts inwards the level of NAIRU will fall. This means that it is now possible to increase aggregate demand, and reduce unemployment, up until NAIRU1 without a rise in inflation.

WHY HAS NAIRU FALLEN?

One of the success stories of UK economic policy in the last ten years has been the fact that both unemployment and inflation have fallen to historically low levels. This has been achieved by reducing the level of NAIRU and shifting the Phillips Curve inwards.

In the last decade, **active labour market strategies** such as the New Deal and the introduction of the Job Seeker's Allowance, have been successful in reducing **structural and frictional** unemployment.

The success of these policies has increased the **potential growth** rate of the economy and shifted the AS curve outwards. There are now more workers employed in the economy and retraining programmes have helped to alleviate skill shortages. This means that, when aggregate demand has been increased to reduce unemployment, there has been greater flexibility in the labour market and, as a result, there has not been upward pressure on wages or inflation. The level of NAIRU has fallen and the economy can now achieve a higher level of growth and employment without inflation.

Chapter 15
THE ECONOMICS OF INTERNATIONAL TRADE

International trade has expanded at a phenomenal rate over the last 50 years. Indeed, the value of world exports now stands at over $6 trillion. The globalisation of the world economy means that most nations are heavily exposed to **trade flows** in goods and services. For countries such as the UK, the performance of its major industries and firms in international markets is crucial to the long-term health of its economy.

WHY DO COUNTRIES TRADE WITH EACH OTHER?

Trade can bring benefits to both consumers and firms, which increases the overall level of **economic welfare**.

1. Trade can lead to an improvement in overall **economic welfare** if countries **specialise** in the products in which they have a **productive advantage.** This concept is explained in greater detail below when we examine the law of comparative advantage.

2. There are some goods that we cannot produce in this country because of inappropriate resources and the wrong climate. Good examples include bananas, bauxite and gold. We need to **export** goods to fund **imports** of these items.

3. Trade allows firms to exploit **economies of scale** (see Chapter 5) by operating in much larger markets. Economies of scale lead to **lower average costs** of production and can be passed onto consumers in the form of **lower prices**. The UK's membership of the EU gives British firms access to an enormous market. The fifteen member nations of the EU have over 370 million consumers with a massive total purchasing power.

4. **International competition** stimulates **higher productive efficiency** (see Chapter 6). Lower average costs should feed through to **lower prices** in the shops and increase **consumer surplus**. Overseas competition can also stop domestic monopolies from exploiting their position.

5. Trade enhances **consumer choice**. When a British consumer purchases a new TV there is a tremendous range of products from which to choose. Without trade, consumers would have a relatively limited choice, which could reduce their welfare.

6. Trade leads to a **faster rate of technological diffusion**. This leads to the development of better quality products for consumers and enhances their overall standard of living.

7. Trade can increase a country's rate of **economic growth**. If an economy has a **current account surplus**, where the value of exports of good and services is greater than the value of imports of goods and services, economic growth will increase. The UK has a current account deficit (see Chapter 16) and trade has, therefore, reduced economic growth.

COMPARATIVE ADVANTAGE AND THE GAINS FROM INTERNATIONAL TRADE

The **law of comparative advantage** suggests that countries should **specialise** and **trade** in the products that they have a comparative advantage in producing.

A **comparative advantage** exists when a country has a **margin of superiority** in the production of a good or service i.e. where the **opportunity cost** of production is lower. By specialising in the production of products where they have a comparative advantage each country can increase their **consumption** and **economic welfare** (under certain assumptions). This concept is explained in the worked example below.

Consider two countries producing two goods – DVD players and mobile phones. If each country allocates 50% of their **economic resources** to the production of DVD players and mobile phones, the **production possibilities** are as shown in the following table.

	DVD Players	Mobile Phones
UK	1000	500
Japan	2400	800
Total Output	**3400**	**1300**

A country has an **absolute advantage** in the production of a good or service if it can produce that product using fewer factors of production than another nation. In this example, Japan has an **absolute advantage** over the UK in the production of both DVD players and mobile phones. This is because with an equal amount of resources allocated to both products, Japan can produce more DVD players and mobile phones.

At first glance it may appear impossible for Japan to benefit from trade if it has an absolute superiority in the production of both goods. However, the law of comparative advantage demonstrates that there are gains from trade even if one nation has an **absolute advantage** over another country in the production of both products.

CALCULATING COMPARATIVE ADVANTAGE

To identify which country should specialise in a particular product we need to analyse the internal **opportunity costs** (see Chapter 1) for each country.

For example, suppose the UK wished to increase the production of mobile phones, the opportunity cost of each extra mobile phone is two DVD players (1000/500). For Japan, the same decision has an opportunity cost of three DVD players (2400/800). Therefore, the **UK has a comparative advantage in mobile phones** because it has to give up fewer DVD players than Japan.

Suppose Japan wished to increase production of DVD players, the opportunity cost of one extra DVD player is 1/3 of a mobile phone (800/2400). For the UK the same decision has an opportunity cost of 1/2 of a mobile phone (500/1000). Thus, **Japan has the comparative advantage in DVD players** because it has to give up fewer mobile phones than the UK.

According to the principle of **comparative advantage**, each country specialises in the products in which it has a relative advantage. If the two countries **specialise completely** the UK's output of mobile phones will rise to 1000 while Japan's production of DVD players will increase to 4800. This will mean that the total output of mobile phones produced by the two countries is 1000. This is less than the 1300 mobile phones that were produced before the two countries specialised. This need not be the case. It is possible to **increase the total output of both products** and this is illustrated below.

Total output of both products will increase if the UK specialises completely in mobile phones while Japan allocates 75% of its resources into DVD players and the remaining 25% into mobile phones. The new output levels would be as follows:

Output after Specialisation	DVD Players	Mobile Phones
UK	0	1000
Japan	3600	400
Total Output (gain after specialisation)	**3600** (+200)	**1400** (+100)

By applying the principle of comparative advantage, total output of DVD players has increased by 200, while production of mobile phones has risen by 100. This represents a gain in **economic welfare**. Although total output has increased, consumers in the UK are unable to purchase DVD players. If trade takes place, not only will total output rise, but **consumption will also increase**.

To trade for the mutual benefit of both nations, each has to agree on an acceptable **rate of exchange** of one product for another. To calculate this figure, we must consider the **internal opportunity cost ratios** for each country. In the UK, the original opportunity cost ratio of DVD players to mobile phones is 2 to 1. In Japan the same opportunity cost ratio is 3 to 1.

If the two countries trade, at the **midpoint of the opportunity cost ratios**, 2.5 DVD players for 1 mobile phone, then both countries will benefit from trade. The UK can now obtain 2.5 DVD players for every mobile phone it produces, whereas before trade it could only obtain two. Japan is also better off as it can now obtain 2/5 of a mobile phone for every DVD it manufactures. In the pre-trade scenario it could only have attained 1/3 of a mobile phone.

When the UK split its resources evenly between DVD players and mobile phones there were 1000 DVD players available for consumption. After specialisation, UK consumers would have been unable to purchase DVD players as the country totally specialised in mobile phones. For specialisation and trade to be beneficial, UK consumers will want to be able to consume more DVD players than they did before the country specialised in producing mobile phones. Let us suppose that the UK imports 1050 DVD players from Japan to achieve this goal. If the two countries trade at a rate of exchange of **2.5 DVD players for 1 mobile phone** the UK must export 420 DVD players to Japan (1050/2.5). The post trade situation is illustrated in the table below. The figures in brackets represent the trade flows between the countries.

Post-Trade Allocation	DVD Players	Mobile Phones
UK	1050 (+1050)	580 (-420)
Japan	2550 (-1050)	820 (+420)
Total Output	**3600**	**1400**

Compared with the pre-specialisation output levels, consumers in both countries now have an increased supply of both goods from which to choose. Total output and consumption has increased, and both countries have benefited from specialisation and trade.

ASSUMPTIONS BEHIND THE LAW OF COMPARATIVE ADVANTAGE

It is important to remember that the law of comparative advantage is based on a number of underlying assumptions:

▶ There are **two countries that produce only two goods** – this assumption is made to keep the explanation as simple as possible, but the model can be applied to the world economy where a wide variety of goods and services are produced.

▶ **Perfect occupational mobility of factors of production** – this means that resources can be easily transferred from mobile phone to DVD player production. For these two products this does not seem to be a particularly unrealistic assumption. However, this may not always be case. It may not be possible to transfer resources between certain types of products; for example, sheep farming and computer chips.

▶ **Constant returns to scale** (i.e. doubling the input leads to a doubling of output) – it is assumed that the opportunity cost ratios stay constant as resources are transferred from one industry to another. If businesses exploit increasing returns to scale (see Chapter 5) when they specialise, the potential gains from trade are much greater. However, if decreasing returns to scale set in the gains from trade may not materialise.

▶ **Zero transportation costs** – if we introduce transport costs into the model, then any comparative advantage a country may have could well be eliminated. The implementation of **tariffs** will have the same effect.

WHAT FACTORS DETERMINE COMPARATIVE ADVANTAGE?

If an economy has a comparative advantage in one good, there is no guarantee that it will last forever. Comparative advantages change all the time. Some businesses enjoy a comparative advantage in one product for several years and then lose this advantage when rival producers from other countries enter their markets.

For a country, the following factors are important in determining the relative costs of production and, therefore, comparative advantage:

- The **quantity and quality of factors of production** available – For example, a country with a larger and more skilled workforce is more likely to have a comparative advantage in the production of manufactured goods.

- **Investment in research & development** – may give a nation's firms cost advantages through the development of superior production techniques. R&D may allow a firm to develop products and techniques that it can patent. This will give these firms a significant advantage in the market place.

- Movements in the **exchange rate** – a country with a lower cost of production may not be able to exploit this relative cost advantage fully as the prices of goods and services in international markets are distorted by the exchange rate. For example, a rise in value of a currency will increase the price of exports on international markets. This might eliminate any relative cost advantage.

- **Long term rates of inflation** – if a country has a higher inflation rate than other countries it will lose competitiveness on international markets. As a result, it may lose its comparative advantage in certain areas.

- **Import controls,** such as tariffs, can be used to create an artificial comparative advantage for a country's domestic producers (see notes below). By raising the price of imports, a government can protect domestic firms from more efficient foreign producers.

- **Non-price competitiveness** of producers – consumers do not just purchase products because they are cheaper than substitutes. Non-price factors such as product design, reliability, quality and after-sales support are also important in determining comparative advantage.

IMPORT CONTROLS AND PROTECTIONISM

Protectionism is a policy that protects domestic firms from overseas competition. The main methods of protection are outlined below:

- **Tariffs – a tariff is a tax on imports** and can be used to **restrict imports** and **raise revenue** for the government. The effects of tariffs on a market are discussed in Chapter 4.

- **Quotas** – are **physical limits** that are placed on the level of imports coming into a country. Quotas can be in terms of volume (number of units imported) or value (value of imports). For example, the EU places a limit of volume of textile imports entering the EU from India.

- **Subsidies** – these are government payments to firms to encourage domestic production. The subsidy lowers the costs of production and makes firms artificially competitive in international markets.

- **Embargoes** – are a total ban on imported goods. These are usually introduced for political or strategic reasons. For example the USA has an embargo on all Cuban products.

- **Voluntary Export Restraint Agreements (VERs)** – these are agreements between counties that limit trade in certain products to a specific quota. For example, Russia has voluntarily agreed to limit its exports of steel to the USA.

- **Administrative Barriers –** countries can make it difficult for firms to import by imposing restrictions and being 'deliberately' bureaucratic. These trade barriers range from **stringent safety and specification checks** to long hold-ups at customs.

ECONOMIC ARGUMENTS FOR PROTECTIONISM

The law of comparative advantage suggests there are significant gains to be had from trade. In reality, however, free trade creates winners and losers. The losers tend to be those nations with poor international competitiveness who cannot compete in global markets. There are a number of economic arguments that can justify the implementation of import controls, and these are examined below:

Infant Industry Argument

Some economists believe that it is possible to select certain industries that possess a **potential comparative advantage.** These industries may have all the necessary economic resources to be successful in international markets, but are not yet able to compete because they have not been able to fully exploit **economies of scale.**

Short-term protection from established foreign competition will allow the **infant industry** to grow and develop its comparative advantage. Once the industry is competitive, the import control can be removed and the product can be left to trade freely in international markets. The danger of this form of protection is that an industry, free of the disciplines of foreign competition, will never achieve full efficiency. It can also be argued that in an ever-changing global marketplace it is very difficult to predict which industries will be successful in the future.

Protection against 'dumping'

Dumping refers to the **sale of a good below its cost of production**. In the short term, consumers benefit from the low prices of the foreign goods but, in the longer term, persistent undercutting of domestic prices will force domestic producers out of business. With no domestic competition the foreign firm may be able to establish itself as a **monopoly**. It would then be in a position to raise its prices and exploit consumers. Import controls on products sold below their cost of production can, therefore, be justified to prevent the long term exploitation of the consumer.

Externalities and Import Controls

Protectionism can also be used to take account of **negative externalities** (see Chapter 7) produced by certain goods and services. Goods such as tobacco, firearms and illegal drugs all have adverse social effects. Protectionism can safeguard society from the importation of these goods, by **imposing high tariffs** or by **banning the importation of the good** altogether.

Non Economic Reasons

Some arguments for protectionism do not always work in the best interests of the world economy. Governments tend to place the protection of their nation's interests above the welfare of the world economy. In this sense many of following policies are driven by a degree of economic nationalism:

▶ Countries may choose not to **over-specialise** in the areas where they possess a comparative advantage. One of the potential dangers of over-specialisation is that unemployment may rise quickly if an industry moves into structural decline as new international competition emerges.

▶ Restriction on imports will improve the **current account balance** (see Chapter 16).

▶ The government may also wish to protect against high levels of imports to **maintain domestic employment** and **boost economic growth.**

▶ Protectionism through the use of tariffs will provide the government with a source of **revenue**.

▶ Protection may also be used to prevent trade with certain countries on **political grounds**. The UK government currently has trade sanctions against Iraq.

PROBLEMS WITH IMPORT PROTECTION

▶ Tariffs can lead to **a deadweight welfare loss** (see Chapter 4).

▶ Consumer welfare is reduced through **higher prices** and restricted **choice**.

▶ Firms that are protected from competition have little incentive to be **productively efficient** (see Chapter 6). This may lead to higher prices for consumers.

▶ The danger with all forms of protectionism is that can lead to **retaliatory action** by other countries. If this retaliation escalates into a trade war, trade volumes will collapse and all countries will suffer.

Chapter 16
THE BALANCE OF PAYMENTS

The Balance of Payments (BOP) records financial transactions between the UK and the international economy. The accounts are split into two sections with the **current account** measuring trade in **goods and services** and the **capital account** tracking **capital flows** in and out of the UK. This includes **capital flows** arising from **foreign direct investment** and **portfolio capital flows** (e.g. share transactions and the buying and selling of Government debt).

THE CURRENT ACCOUNT

The current account primarily measures net trade in goods and services.

Trade in goods includes items such as:
- Manufactured goods
- Semi-finished goods and components
- Energy products
- Raw materials
- Consumer goods and capital goods

Trade in services includes:
- Banking, insurance and consultancy
- Tourism
- Transport and shipping
- Education
- Cultural arts

The current account records the **flow of money** between countries not the movement of goods and services. For example, the sale of a UK produced car to France (an export) would result in a flow of money into the UK, and this would, therefore, be represented as a **plus sign** in the BOP. The fact that the car leaves the UK is irrelevant. Similarly if a UK consumer buys insurance from a German firm (an import), this would result in a flow of money out of the UK and would be represented as a **minus sign** in the BOP.

There are two main elements in the current account:

▶ The **trade in goods section**, or visible balance, records trade in tangible products. Over the majority of the last 20 years the UK has had a **visible deficit**. This means that the **value of imported goods** exceeds the **value of exported goods**. For example, if the value of imported goods is £100bn and the value of exported goods is £70bn, then the trade in goods, or visible deficit, would be £30bn.

▶ The **trade in services section**, or invisible balance, measures trade in intangible services. The UK has traditionally experienced an **invisible surplus**. This means that the **value of exported services** exceeds the **value of imported services**. For example, if the value of exported services is £50bn and the value of imported services is £40bn, then the trade in services, or invisible surplus, would be £10bn.

At AS Level, students could explain these two sections and highlight that they combine to give the **current account balance**. During the majority of the last 20 years the UK has had a **current account deficit**. This occurs when the **value of imported goods and services** exceeds the **value of exported goods and services**.

At A2 Level, candidates should explain that the current account includes two additional sections:

1. **Net income** measures two main flows of income into and out of the UK: the **compensation of employees** and **investment income**.

▶ The **compensation of employees** relates to flows of **wages and salaries**. For example, the wages and salaries earned by UK residents while working abroad represent a flow of money into the UK, while a salary earned by a German resident while working in London would represent an outflow of money.

▶ **Investment income** is the same as **net property income from abroad** (NPIA). This was explained in Chapter 8. **NPIA** is the net balance of **interest, profits and dividends (IPD)** coming into the UK from UK assets owned overseas matched against the outflow of profits and other income from foreign owned assets located within the UK. For example, if a British resident receives interest from savings held in a German bank then this would represent an inflow of money to the UK. Similarly, when a Japanese shareholder, who has invested in the UK stockmarket, takes their dividend back to Japan this would represent an outflow of money.

2. **Net current transfers** relate to transfers of money between countries by central government and other economic agents. The UK is a net contributor to EU institutions and these flows of money between the UK and the EU are the most significant component of this section of the current account. Other items classified as net transfers include foreign aid, military grants and money transfers. For example, when a UK resident living abroad sends money back to family in the UK, or pays tax to the Inland Revenue, this would be classed as a net transfer into the UK.

The table below shows how the current account balance was calculated in 2001.

Component	£bn
Trade in goods balance	-33.6
Trade in services balance	+11.1
Net Income	+9.3
Net current transfers	-7.2
Current account balance	-20.4

THE CAPITAL ACCOUNT

Following changes to the measurement of the balance of payments in the late 1990s, **the capital account is now a relatively insignificant component of the accounts**. It includes capital transfers, such as aid given to foreign countries for capital projects, and the acquisition and disposal of non-produced, non-financial assets such as land, copyrights and patents.

THE FINANCIAL ACCOUNT

This is a **new section of the accounts** and, before the re-classification, was known as the capital account. It is primarily concerned with investment flows into and out of the country. The two main components of the financial account are:

Direct investment flows – these relate to flows of **foreign direct investment**. For example, when Nissan invested money in the car plant at Sunderland this would have represented an inflow of direct investment to the UK. Similarly, when BP invests money in overseas oilfields this will result in an outflow of direct investment from the UK.

Portfolio investment flows – consider the sale and purchase of **UK shares** and **government securities**. For example, when an overseas investor buys shares on the UK stock market, there will be an inflow of portfolio investment. When overseas investors sell shares or securities, there is an outflow.

There are other smaller sections of the financial account that examine trades in **financial derivatives and reserve assets.** The reserve assets section includes trades in gold and foreign exchange reserves held by the Bank of England.

WHY THE BALANCE OF PAYMENTS SHOULD BALANCE

In theory, the **balance of payments should always balance**. The sum of the current account, capital account and financial account balances should be **zero**. In reality however, this is never the case. This is because it is impossible to record accurately every single transaction that takes place between the UK and the rest of the world. An additional item known as **net errors or omissions**, or the balancing item, is added to the balance of payments to ensure that the accounts balance. This figure is a statistical adjustment to account for transactions that are missed or incorrectly recorded.

A summary of the overall balance of payments for 2001 is shown overleaf.

Component	£bn
Current account balance	-20.4
Capital account balance	+1.5
Financial account balance	+19.2
Net errors or omissions	+0.3
Overall balance of payments	**zero**

If a country has a **current account deficit** it will need a **surplus** on its **capital and financial account.** One way of doing this is to attract banking flows, or **hot money,** into the economy. Higher interest rates will make it more attractive for overseas investors to place their money into UK bank and building society accounts. In a world of **capital mobility**, providing that a country is perceived as creditworthy, it should not be too much of a problem for an economy to finance a current account deficit.

ECONOMIC GROWTH AND THE CURRENT ACCOUNT

Normally, as economic growth increases and domestic incomes rise, we expect to see an **increased demand for imports.** This can come from both consumers and firms. The extent to which imports rise when incomes grow is measured by the **income elasticity of demand for imports**. This examines the responsiveness of the demand for imports to a change in consumers' income. It gives us an idea of the **marginal propensity to import (mpm)** which, of course, is a concept used when calculating the **multiplier** (see Chapter 8). If the **mpm** is high, then imports will rise quickly when the economy experiences economic growth. Unless there is a corresponding rise in the volume of exports sold overseas the **current account balance will worsen**.

THE BALANCE OF PAYMENTS AND LIVING STANDARDS

A common misconception is that current account deficits are always bad for the economy. This is not necessarily true. In the short term, if a country is importing a high volume of goods and services then this can boost **living standards**. It allows consumers to buy a higher level of **consumer durables** and other items. However, in the long term a current account deficit may be a symptom of a weakening domestic economy and **a lack of international competitiveness**. If imports continue to rise, this will threaten domestic employment and incomes and **living standards may fall**.

CAUSES OF A CURRENT ACCOUNT DEFICIT

By definition, if some economies are running current account deficits, then others must be running surpluses. It is important to identify the underlying causes of a current account deficit before designing policies to correct the problem. Some of the more common causes of a current account deficit are:

▶ **High level of economic growth** – In a boom, when consumption and investment expenditure tend to rise, it is inevitable that some of this increased spending will leave the country as consumers and firms purchase imports. Other things being equal, this will cause the **current account balance to deteriorate**. The higher the marginal propensity to import, the greater the increase in imports will be.

▶ **Lack of productive capacity of domestic firms** – If home producers have insufficient capacity to meet rising demand from consumers then imports of goods and services will come into the country to satisfy this excess demand. As a result, the current account will worsen.

▶ **Poor price and non-price competitiveness** – Competitiveness can be measured by cost levels and domestic prices relative to international competitors, but non-price factors are also important. These include quality, design, reliability and after-sales service. In Chapter 13, inflation was seen to be a key determinant of international competitiveness. If the UK has higher inflation than the rest of the world it will lose competitiveness in international markets. Assuming that the quality of goods and services and the exchange rate remain unchanged, the rise in relative inflation will reduce UK exports and increase import penetration, and result in a deterioration of the current account.

- **Declining comparative advantage in many areas** – The advantages that countries have in producing certain goods and services can change over time, as technology alters and other countries exploit their economic resources and develop competing industries. The UK manufacturing sector, for example, has suffered over the last 25 years from the emergence of low cost production in newly industrialised countries.

- **An over valued exchange rate** – Some economists believe that current account deficits stem from the exchange rate being at too high a level. A high exchange rate causes export prices to be higher in foreign markets whilst imports become relatively cheaper. Other things being equal, this will cause imports to rise, exports to fall and the current account balance to worsen.

- **Falling surplus in an important mineral resource** – some countries rely heavily on the export of specific primary commodities whose prices on international markets might be highly volatile. A fall in price when demand from purchasers is inelastic can cause a sharp fall in total export revenues and a sudden deterioration in a country's current account.

POLICIES TO SOLVE A CURRENT ACCOUNT DEFICIT

There are two main groups of policies designed to reduce the scale of a current account deficit:

1. EXPENDITURE REDUCING POLICIES

These policies aim to **reduce the spending of consumers and firms** so that the demand for imports falls. The following policies could be introduced:

- **Higher income taxes** will reduce real disposable incomes and should lead to a fall in expenditure on imports.

- **Higher interest rates** will discourage borrowing, increase saving and reduce consumers' real 'effective' disposable incomes. This should lead to a fall in consumer spending and a reduction in the level of imports.

The problem with these policies is that they only provide a **short term solution** and do not tackle the underlying causes of a current account deficit. They also reduce aggregate demand and this will result in **lower economic growth and higher unemployment**.

2. EXPENDITURE SWITCHING POLICIES

These are policies that attempt to encourage consumers to **switch** their demand away from imports and towards the output of domestic firms. This occurs if the **relative price** of imports can be raised, or if the relative price of UK products can be lowered. This should then cause a change in the spending patterns of consumers away from foreign goods and towards output produced within the domestic economy. The following policies might achieve this goal:

- The introduction of **tariffs** (see Chapter 4) or other import controls (see Chapter 15).

- Policies that **reduce the rate of inflation** in the economy below that of other international competitors (see Chapter 13).

- Measures that **reduce unit costs** of domestic firms making their output relatively cheaper. (e.g. measures to encourage **higher investment and labour productivity**).

- A **devaluation** or **depreciation** of the exchange rate will reduce the price of exports and increase the price of imports. This should stimulate foreign demand for exports and encourage UK consumers to purchase fewer imports and more home produced products. Other things being equal, the current account balance will improve.

At A2 Level, students must be able to explain why, in the short term, a **depreciation** of the exchange rate may not improve the current account. This is due to the **low price elasticity of demand** for imports and exports in the immediate aftermath of an exchange rate change. Diagram 14. 1 illustrates this possibility.

Assume that the economy starts at position A with a substantial current account deficit. If there is then a fall in the value of the exchange rate, initially the volume of imports will remain steady because contracts for imported goods and services will have already been signed. However, the depreciation raises the Sterling price of imports and, as a result, **total spending on imports will rise**.

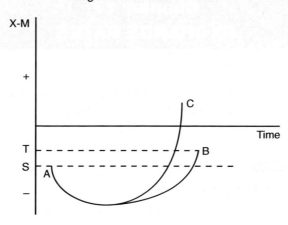

Diagram 16.1: The 'J Curve'

At the same time, demand for exports will not change significantly because existing export contracts will have also been signed. The fall in the exchange rate reduces the price of exports and, as a result, **total spending on exports may fall** if the demand for exports is inelastic. Thus, in the short term, **the current account deficit may worsen**.

Providing that the combined **elasticities of demand for imports and exports** are greater than one in the longer term then the current account balance will improve over time. This is known as the **Marshall-Lerner condition**. Once firms begin to sign new contracts that take into account the relative price changes following the fall in the value of the exchange rate, there will be a significant change in import and export volumes. This will result in a fall in spending on imports and a rise in spending on exports. Thus, in the **long term**, the **current account balance will improve**.

In Diagram 16.1, the current account deficit falls by distance ST at point B. If the elasticities of demand for imports and exports are much higher then the current deficit may be transformed into a surplus. This is shown by the curve AC.

It is important to remember that a depreciation of the exchange rate will not normally be enough on its own to correct a current account deficit. This is particularly the case if the causes of the deficit are long term and structural. Other policies are required that improve the **supply-side performance** of the economy and make domestically produced goods and services more competitive in international markets.

The key to controlling a current account deficit in the long term is for the economy to achieve **relatively low inflation** with sufficient **productive capacity** to meet the domestic demand from consumers. This requires a period of low inflation, low interest rates and a competitive exchange rate matched with sufficient **non-price competitiveness** in overseas markets.

Chapter 17
EXCHANGE RATES

The exchange rate measures the **international value of Sterling** in terms of how much international currency it will buy. The market value of the pound is determined on a daily basis in the **foreign exchange markets** (FOREX) where billions of £s worth of currencies are traded every hour.

EXCHANGE RATE SYSTEMS

The UK operates in a **managed exchange rate** system:

▶ The value of the exchange rate is primarily determined by the **demand and supply** for Sterling on the foreign exchange market.

▶ The government regards the exchange rate as one of its key policy tools.

▶ Official intervention by the Bank of England and changes in domestic interest rates can be used to influence the value of the currency.

The members of the EU that have adopted the **Euro** operate in a **fixed exchange rate** system:

▶ This means that all countries within the system are committed to a **single fixed exchange rate**. It is important to remember that the value of the Euro can fluctuate with currencies outside the 'Eurozone', such as the Dollar and the Yen.

▶ All countries within the system have the **same interest rate**.

▶ National central banks have, therefore, **lost autonomy** over monetary and exchange rate policy.

MEASURING THE EXCHANGE RATE:

Currencies are traded around the world in a truly **global market**. The scale of currency transactions is enormous. Over $1,500 billion worth of currency is bought and sold each day on the world's foreign exchange markets. Not all currency traded is used to finance international trade in goods and services. A substantial proportion is simply speculative buying and selling and, as a result, this can create widespread currency volatility.

Exchange rate prices are expressed in various ways:

1. The **spot exchange rate** is the actual exchange rate for a currency at a particular moment in time. This is determined by the FOREX market, on a minute by minute basis, and is dependent on the flow of demand and supply for any one particular currency. The value of currency is usually expressed as a **bilateral exchange rate**. This is simply the rate at which one currency trades against another. Examples of bilateral exchange rates include:

   • the Sterling/Dollar exchange rate (£/$).
   • the Dollar/Yen exchange rate ($/YEN).
   • the Sterling/Euro exchange rate £/€. This rate has been quoted since the launch of the Euro in January 1999.

2. The **forward exchange rate** involves the delivery of currency at some time in the future at an agreed rate. Companies wanting to reduce the risk of exchange rate uncertainty often buy their currency at the forward rate for delivery in three or six months time.

3. The **effective exchange rate** or **Sterling index** is a weighted index of Sterling's value against a basket of international currencies. The proportion of trade between the UK and each country determines the size of the weights.

THE DEMAND FOR AND SUPPLY OF A CURRENCY

In the UK, the twin forces of demand and supply are the main determinants of the market value of the currency. When a currency is in strong demand, it will **appreciate** in value. In contrast, when there is large scale selling, the currency will **depreciate**. The demand and supply of a currency are determined by the following factors:

Demand for a currency
- exports of goods
- exports of services
- inflows of direct investment
- inflows of portfolio investment and speculative demand for the currency
- official buying of the currency by the Central Bank

Supply of a currency
- imports of goods
- imports of services
- outflows of direct investment
- outflows of portfolio investment and speculative selling of the currency
- official selling of the currency by the Central Bank

In Diagram 17.1, the equilibrium exchange rate for the pound and the US dollar (£/$) is at price P, where supply and demand for sterling are equal.

If there is an **increase in demand** for the pound, due to a surge in exports to the USA, there will be **upward pressure** on the value of the exchange rate. In Diagram 17.2, the demand for Sterling will shift to the right from D0 to D1 and the value of the pound will appreciate from P0 to P1. Conversely, if there is a fall in demand for Sterling, perhaps due to a fall in foreign direct investment from the USA, the demand for Sterling will shift from D0 to D2 and the currency will depreciate from P0 to P2.

An increased supply of pounds, due to a rise in imports from the USA, will apply downward pressure on the value of the currency. In Diagram 17.3, the supply of Sterling will shift to the right from S0 to S1 and the value of the pound will depreciate from P0 to P1. Conversely, if there is a fall in supply for Sterling, perhaps due to a fall in speculative selling of the currency, the supply of Sterling will shift from S0 to S2 and the currency will appreciate from P0 to P2.

In today's highly liquid foreign exchange rate markets, where billions of dollars worth of currencies change hands every working day, it is important to recognise that **trade flows** between countries are not as important as **capital flows** in determining a currency's value. In the case of the UK/USA exchange rate for example, trade between the two nations is vast, but is dwarfed by speculative buying and selling and inflows and outflows of portfolio and direct investment.

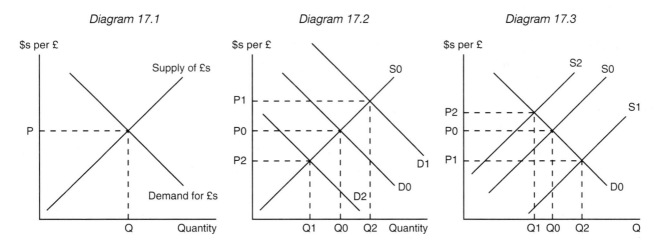

Diagram 17.1   *Diagram 17.2*   *Diagram 17.3*

KEY FACTORS THAT DRIVE A CURRENCY IN THE FOREIGN EXCHANGE RATE MARKETS

MONETARY POLICY: Changes in interest rates can have a significant effect on the exchange rate. In a world where financial capital moves freely between countries a **rise in interest rates** may cause the currency to **appreciate**. If a nation's interest rates increase, and are higher than in other countries, there is likely to be an **inflow** of speculative **'hot money'** to take advantage of the higher return on saving. This will boost the demand for the currency and can cause the exchange rate to appreciate.

ECONOMIC GROWTH: Countries that suffer a prolonged recession often find that their exchange rate will weaken. The foreign exchange markets may see slow economic growth as a sign of economic weakness and mark down the value of the currency.

When economic growth is above trend, there is a danger that **demand pull inflation** will emerge (see Chapter 13). The monetary authorities may decide to raise interest rates to control aggregate demand. This rise in rates will make the currency more attractive to foreign investors looking for a good rate of return.

INFLATION: The theory of purchasing power parity (PPP) explains how changes in domestic prices can influence the exchange rate. The theory states that the exchange rate between two countries is in equilibrium when the price of an identical basket of goods and services is the same in both nations. For example, suppose the price of a hamburger in the USA is $2 while the cost of the same hamburger in the UK is £1. If £1 = $2, then the exchange rate is in equilibrium because the price of the hamburger is the same in both countries.

If UK prices accelerate at a faster rate than in the USA, the exchange rate will no longer be in equilibrium. The theory of purchasing power parity suggests that the exchange rate should adjust so that the price of a basket of goods and services is identical in both the UK and the USA. This means that the pound must depreciate against the dollar.

Going back to our hamburger example, suppose the price of a hamburger in the USA remains at $2, but the price of a UK hamburger increases to £1.50. For the hamburger to be the same price in both countries the pound must **depreciate**. The equilibrium exchange rate would now be £1 = $1.33 ($2/£1.5). A rise in UK prices has led to a fall in the value of the currency. Therefore, those countries with higher than average inflation should see their exchange rate fall in the long run.

TRADE: Selling exports creates a demand for a currency from foreign importers. Buying imports increases the supply of currency, as domestic importers have to sell the domestic currency to buy foreign currencies. When an economy is running a **current account deficit**, there will be **downward pressure on the exchange rate** as there is a net supply of the currency (the supply of currency exceeds demand). Indeed a **depreciation** of the currency may be required as an **expenditure-switching policy** to correct the current account deficit. If a country is running a **current account surplus** there is a net demand for the currency and the exchange rate should **appreciate**.

FISCAL POLICY: The foreign exchange markets consider a government's fiscal policy and, in particular, how much it is having to borrow to be a key economic indicator. Countries with very strong public sector finances (a large budget surplus) may see their currency appreciate.

SPECULATION AND SPECIAL FACTORS: The power of speculators in foreign exchange markets is enormous. The effects of speculation and special factors (political events, natural disasters and changing commodity prices) should not be underestimated.

ECONOMIC EFFECTS OF EXCHANGE RATE MOVEMENTS

A depreciation in the value of Sterling will have wide-ranging economic effects:

Exports
▶ Exporters should benefit from a fall in the value of the pound. UK goods will be cheaper when priced in a foreign currency and, as a result, demand for UK **exports should rise**.

▶ The effect on the demand for exports is determined by the foreign price elasticity of demand for UK goods.

▶ Exporting firms may decide to hold export prices constant and increase their profit margins.

Imports
▶ A depreciation in Sterling will make imports more expensive and, as a result, the demand for **imports should fall**.

Balance of Payments
▶ Normally a depreciation will **improve the current account balance**. The demand for imports will fall and the demand for exports will rise. However in the short term, if the Marshall-Lerner condition is not satisfied there may be a '**J curve' effect** and the current account will deteriorate (see Chapter 16).

Inflation
▶ A fall in the exchange rate increases import prices in the UK.

▶ Higher prices for imported components and raw materials may lead to **cost push inflation** (see Chapter 13). The extent to which firms raise their prices depends on the price elasticity of demand for the product.

Economic Growth & Employment
▶ Higher exports and falling imports will **increase aggregate demand and GDP**.

▶ A rise in aggregate demand should reduce **demand deficient unemployment**.

▶ An appreciation of the exchange rate is likely to have the opposite effects to those described above. Remember that changes in the exchange rate will have a lagged effect on the economy and will not happen instantaneously.